Rick Steves

POCKET

AMSTERDAM

Rick Steves & Gene Openshaw

D0905804

Contents

Introduction

Amsterdam of the Golden Age (the 1600s) was the world's richest city. And it's still a wonderland of canals, stately brick mansions, and carillons chiming from church spires. Today's Amsterdam is a progressive place of 850,000 people and almost as many bikes. Visitors will find no end of world-class sights: Van Gogh's *Sunflowers,* Rembrandt's self-portraits, and Anne Frank's secret hiding place.

Enjoy the city's intimate charms. Stroll quiet neighborhoods, browse bookshops, sample exotic foods, and let a local show you the right way to swallow a pickled herring. With legal marijuana and prostitution, Amsterdam exudes an earthy spirit of live and let live. Consider yourself warned...or titillated. Take it all in, then pause to watch the clouds blow past gabled rooftops—and see the Golden Age reflected in a quiet canal.

Amsterdam

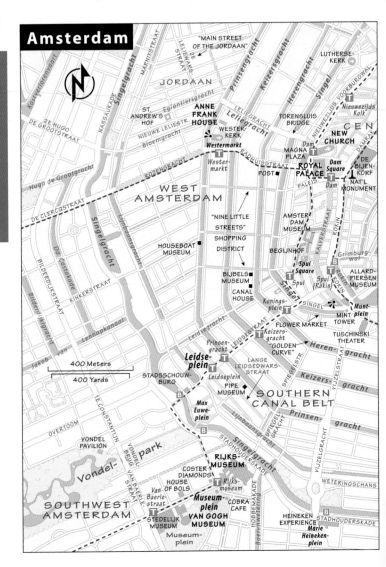

"MAIN STREET OF THE JORDAAN"

LUTHERSE-KERK

JORDAAN

ST. ANDREW'S HOF

ANNE FRANK HOUSE

WESTER-KERK

Westermarkt

TORENSLUIS BRIDGE

Nieuwezijds Kolk

NEW CHURCH

CEN

MAGNA PLAZA

DE BIJEN-KORF

ROYAL PALACE

Dam Square

POST

WEST AMSTERDAM

NAT'L MONUMENT

"NINE LITTLE STREETS" SHOPPING DISTRICT

AMSTER-DAM MUSEUM

HOUSEBOAT MUSEUM

BEGIJNHOF

Spui Square

ALLARD-PIERSEN MUSEUM

BIJBELS MUSEUM

CANAL HOUSE

Spui

Spui (Rokin)

Kaningsplein

MINT TOWER

FLOWER MARKET

TUSCHINSKI THEATER

Prinsengracht

"GOLDEN CURVE"

LANGE LEIDSEDWARS-STRAAT

Leidseplein

Leidseplein

STADSSCHOUW-BURG

PIPE MUSEUM

SOUTHERN CANAL BELT

Max Euwe-plein

400 Meters

400 Yards

VONDEL PAVILION

VONDEL-park

RIJKS-MUSEUM

COSTER DIAMONDS

HOUSE OF BOLS

Rijks-museum

COBRA CAFE

Museum-plein

Van Baerle-straat

SOUTHWEST AMSTERDAM

STEDELIJK MUSEUM

VAN GOGH MUSEUM

Museum-plein

HEINEKEN EXPERIENCE

Marie Heineken-plein

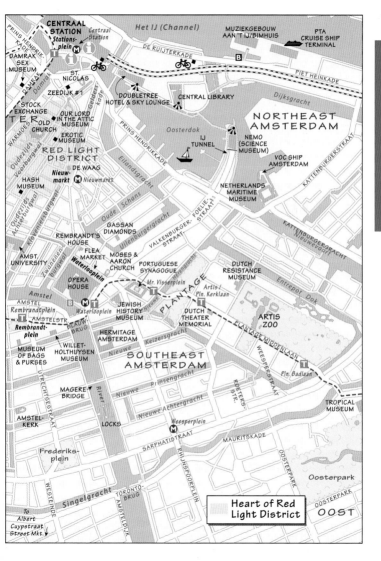

Het IJ (Channel)

CENTRAAL STATION
Stationsplein
Centraal Station

MUZIEKGEBOUW AAN 'T IJ/BIMHUIS

PTA CRUISE SHIP TERMINAL

PRINS HENDRIKKADE
DE RUIJTERKADE
PIET HEINKADE

DAMRAK SEX MUSEUM

ST. NICOLAS
ZEEDIJK #1

DOUBLETREE HOTEL & SKY LOUNGE

CENTRAL LIBRARY

Dijksgracht

STOCK EXCHANGE
OUR LORD IN THE ATTIC MUSEUM
OLD CHURCH
EROTIC MUSEUM

Oosterdok

IJ TUNNEL

NEMO (SCIENCE MUSEUM)

NORTHEAST AMSTERDAM

VOC SHIP AMSTERDAM

RED LIGHT DISTRICT

DE WAAG
Nieuwmarkt

PRINS HENDRIKKADE

Eilandsgracht

NETHERLANDS MARITIME MUSEUM

KATTENBURGERSTRAAT

HASH MUSEUM

Oude Schans

GASSAN DIAMONDS

Uilenburgergracht
VALKENBURGER- STRAAT
FOELIE- STRAAT

KATTENBURGERGRACHT
Nieuwevaart

REMBRANDT'S HOUSE
FLEA MARKET
Waterlooplein
MOSES & AARON CHURCH
PORTUGUESE SYNAGOGUE

DUTCH RESISTANCE MUSEUM

Entrepot Dok

AMST. UNIVERSITY

OPERA HOUSE

Mr. Visserplein
Artis / Pln. Kerklaan

PLANTAGE

AMSTEL
Rembrandtplein

Waterlooplein

JEWISH HISTORY MUSEUM

DUTCH THEATER MEMORIAL

ARTIS ZOO

AMSTELSTR.
Rembrandt-plein

HERMITAGE AMSTERDAM

PLANTAGE MIDDENLAAN

MUSEUM OF BAGS & PURSES

WILLET-HOLTHUYSEN MUSEUM

Keizersgracht

SOUTHEAST AMSTERDAM

WEESPERSTRAAT

Pln. Badlaan

MAGERE BRIDGE

Nieuwe Prinsengracht

Nieuwe Achtergracht

ROETERS-STR.

TROPICAL MUSEUM

AMSTEL-KERK

LOCKS

Weesperplein

MAURITSKADE

Frederiksplein

SARPHATISTRAAT

RHIJNSPOORPLEIN

OOSTERPARK

Oosterpark

Singelgracht

TORONTO-BRUG
AMSTELDIJK

To Albert Cuypstraat Street Mkt.

OOST

Heart of Red Light District

About This Book

Rick Steves Pocket Amsterdam is a personal tour guide...in your pocket. The core of the book is six self-guided tours that zero in on Amsterdam's greatest sights and neighborhoods. The Amsterdam City Walk takes you through the heart of the city, giving you the lay of the land. At the Rijksmuseum and Van Gogh Museum, you'll see all the essentials with time left over for browsing. You'll tour the racy Red Light District, meander the tree-lined canals of the Jordaan, and visit the tragic yet uplifting Anne Frank House.

The rest of this book is a traveler's tool kit, with my best advice on how to save money, plan your time, ride public transportation, and avoid lines at the busiest sights. You'll also get recommendations on hotels, restaurants, and activities.

Amsterdam by Neighborhood

Think of Amsterdam as a series of neighborhoods cradling major landmarks. Amsterdam's Centraal Station sits on the north edge of the city. From here, the city spreads out like a fan in a series of concentric canals. Damrak is the main north-south axis, connecting Centraal Station with Dam Square, the city's main square. Farther south are Leidseplein (nightlife) and the major museums (Rijksmuseum and Van Gogh).

To walk north-south through the sightseeing core—from Centraal Station to Dam Square to Leidseplein to the Rijksmuseum—takes about an hour.

Central Amsterdam—the historic core—runs north-south from Centraal Station along Damrak, passing through two major city squares (Dam and Spui) and ending at the Mint Tower. The central spine of streets (Damrak, Kalverstraat, Rokin) has some of the city's main department, chain, and tourist stores. Flanking Damrak on the east is the Red Light District and the revitalized waterfront around the train station.

West Amsterdam lies west of Damrak—from Dam Square to the Anne Frank House. This pleasant area is famous for its four grand canals—named Singel (the original moat), Herengracht (Gentleman's Canal), Keizersgracht (Emperor's Canal), and Prinsengracht (Prince's Canal)—that circle the historic core. West Amsterdam has tree-lined canals fronted by old, gabled mansions, as well as many of my recommended accommodations and restaurants. Within West Amsterdam

Amsterdam's Neighborhoods

is the boutique shopping district known as the Nine Little Streets. Farther west is the quieter, cozier Jordaan neighborhood—good for a stroll, though it's mostly residential. And to the north the old "Haarlem dike"—Haarlemmerstraat and Haarlemmerdijk—is emerging as a trendy, youthful zone for shopping and eating.

The **Southern Canal Belt**—the next ring of canals south of the historic core—is spacious and dotted sparsely with a few intimate museums, art galleries, and antique shops along Nieuwe Spiegelstraat, plus recommended B&Bs. Rowdy Leidseplein anchors the lower corner.

Southwest Amsterdam is defined by two main features: museums and a city park. The city's major art museums (Rijksmuseum, Van Gogh, and Stedelijk) and other sights cluster together on an

▲▲▲**Rijksmuseum** Best collection anywhere of the Dutch Masters—Rembrandt, Hals, Vermeer, and Steen—in a spectacular setting. **Hours:** Daily 9:00-17:00. See page 37.

▲▲▲**Van Gogh Museum** More than 200 paintings by the angst-ridden artist. **Hours:** Daily April-Aug 9:00-19:00, Fri until 21:00, Sat until 18:00 (April-June) and 21:00 (July-Aug); Sept-Oct 9:00-18:00, Fri until 21:00; Nov-March 9:00-17:00, Fri until 21:00. See page 55.

▲▲▲**Anne Frank House** Young Anne's hideaway during the Nazi occupation. **Hours:** April-Oct daily 9:00-22:00; Nov-March Mon-Fri 9:00-20:00, Sat until 22:00, Sun until 19:00. See page 105.

▲▲**Stedelijk Museum** The Netherlands' top modern-art museum. **Hours:** Daily 10:00-18:00, Fri until 22:00. See page 121.

▲▲**Amsterdam Museum** City's growth from fishing village to trading capital to today, including some Rembrandts and a playable carillon. **Hours:** Daily 10:00-17:00. See page 130.

▲▲**Our Lord in the Attic Museum** Catholic church hidden in the attic of a 17th-century merchant's house. **Hours:** Mon-Sat 10:00-18:00, Sun from 13:00. See page 130.

▲▲**Red Light District Walk** Women of the world's oldest profession on the job. **Hours:** Best from noon into the evening; avoid late at night. See page 71.

▲▲**Netherlands Maritime Museum** Rich seafaring story of the Netherlands, told with vivid artifacts. **Hours:** Daily 9:00-17:00. See page 132.

expansive square, Museumplein. The museums are just a short walk from Vondelpark, Amsterdam's version of a central park. While it's less central to stay in Southwest Amsterdam, I've recommended accommodations that are a quick, convenient walk to the area's tram lines.

Southeast Amsterdam contains the former Jewish Quarter and the Jewish Historical Museum. Several sights can be found around the square known as Waterlooplein (Rembrandt's House and

▲▲**Hermitage Amsterdam** Russia's Czarist treasures, on loan from St. Petersburg. **Hours:** Daily 10:00-17:00. See page 135.

▲▲**Dutch Resistance Museum** History of the Dutch struggle against the Nazis. **Hours:** Mon-Fri 10:00-17:00, Sat-Sun from 11:00. See page 137.

▲**Royal Palace** Lavish City Hall that takes you back to the Golden Age of the 17th century. **Hours:** Daily 10:00-17:00 when not closed for official ceremonies. See page 128.

▲**Begijnhof** Quiet courtyard lined with picturesque houses. **Hours:** Daily 8:00-17:30. See page 28.

▲**Hash, Marijuana, and Hemp Museum** All the dope, from history and science to memorabilia. **Hours:** Daily 10:00-22:00. See page 87.

▲**EYE Film Institute Netherlands** Film museum and cinema complex housed in a futuristic building. **Hours:** Exhibits open daily 10:00-19:00, cinemas and bar open roughly 10:00-24:00. See page 133.

▲**Rembrandt's House** The master's reconstructed house, displaying his etchings. **Hours:** Daily 10:00-18:00. See page 134.

▲**Willet-Holthuysen Museum** Elegant 17th-century house. **Hours:** Mon-Fri 10:00-17:00, Sat-Sun from 11:00. See page 125.

▲**Jewish Historical Museum and Portuguese Synagogue** Exhibits on Judaism and culture and beloved synagogue that serves today's Jewish community. **Hours:** Museum daily 11:00-17:00; synagogue Sat-Thu 10:00-17:00, Fri until 15:00 or 16:00. See page 136.

▲**Dutch Theater** Moving memorial in former Jewish detention center. **Hours:** Daily 11:00-17:00. See page 137.

a flea market). Additional sights are gathered in a park-dotted area called the Plantage (Dutch Resistance Museum, a theater-turned-Holocaust-memorial, a zoo, and a botanical garden). Rembrandtplein, another nightlife center, is a five-minute walk away. The short but appealing street called Staalstraat, which connects this area with Rokin in the center, is a delightful place to browse trendy shops.

Northeast Amsterdam has the Netherlands Maritime Museum, Amsterdam's Central Library, and a children's science museum (NEMO).

North Amsterdam, which sits across the very wide IJ (pronounced "eye") waterway, was long neglected as a sleepy residential zone. But recently it has sprouted some interesting restaurant and nightlife options, thanks partly to the construction of the EYE Film Institute and the A'DAM Tower. There are easy, free connections across the river on a public ferry just behind Centraal Station.

Planning Your Time

Amsterdam is worth a full day on even the busiest itinerary and can easily fill three full sightseeing days. The following plan gives you an idea of how much an organized, motivated, and caffeinated person can see.

Day 1: Follow my self-guided Amsterdam City Walk, leading from the train station to Leidseplein, via the quiet Begijnhof, the Amsterdam Museum (make time to tour this), and the flower market. After lunch, visit Amsterdam's two outstanding art museums, located next to each other: the Van Gogh Museum and the Rijksmuseum. In the evening, stroll the Red Light District for some memorable window-shopping.

Day 2: Start your day with a one-hour canal boat tour. Then visit the sights of your choice around Rembrandtplein (Rembrandt's House, Waterlooplein flea market—closed Sun, Gassan Diamonds polishing demo, Dutch Resistance Museum). In the late afternoon, tour the Anne Frank House (reserve two months in advance), then take my self-guided Jordaan Walk before enjoying dinner in that neighborhood.

Day 3: Use this day to browse the wide variety of Amsterdam's museums—the Our Lord in the Attic, Royal Palace, Stedelijk, Bags and Purses, Pipe, and Houseboat.

The Begijnhof still shelters single women.

Flower markets burst with color and scents.

⌂ Stick This Guidebook in Your Ear!

My free Rick Steves Audio Europe app makes it easy to download my audio tours of many of Europe's top attractions. In this book, these include my Amsterdam City Walk, Red Light District Walk, and Jordaan Walk. Audio tours are marked in this book with this symbol: ⌂. It's all free! For more info, see www.ricksteves.com/audioeurope.

With More Time: There are plenty of other small museums to visit in Amsterdam—find suggestions in the Sights chapter. Or day-trip to nearby towns such as Haarlem, Delft, or Edam.

When to Go

Although Amsterdam can be crowded in summer, it's a great time to visit, with long days, lively festivals, and sunny weather (rarely too hot for comfort). Amsterdam can also be busy—with higher hotel prices—in late March, April, and May, when the tulip fields are in full bloom. Fall comes with lighter crowds, though conferences can drive up prices. Spring and fall have generally mild weather. Amsterdam in winter (late Oct-mid-March) is cold and rainy, but the city feels lively, not touristy.

Before You Go

You'll have a smoother trip if you tackle a few things ahead of time. For more information on these topics, see the Practicalities chapter (and www.ricksteves.com).

Make sure your passport is valid. If it's due to expire within six months of your ticketed date of return, you need to renew it (www.travel.state.gov).

Arrange your transportation. Book your international flights early. If you're traveling beyond Amsterdam, research rail passes, train reservations, and car rentals.

Book rooms well in advance, especially if your trip falls during the peak season (summer) or any major holidays or festivals.

Plan your strategy for Amsterdam's top sights. Buy tickets online in advance for the most popular museums: the Rijksmuseum, Van Gogh, and Anne Frank House. Tickets to the Van Gogh Museum are likely available online only (no in-person ticket sales). Because Anne Frank House tickets often sell out, it's smart to buy them two months in advance. More details are in each tour chapter.

Call your bank. Alert your bank that you'll be using your debit and credit cards in Europe. Ask about transaction fees and daily withdrawal limits, and get the PIN number for your credit card. You don't need to bring euros for your trip; you can withdraw euros from cash machines in Europe. Some travelers carry a third card as a backup.

Use your smartphone smartly. Sign up for an international service plan to reduce your costs, or rely on Wi-Fi in Europe instead. Download any apps you'll want on the road, such as maps, translation, transit, and Rick Steves Audio Europe.

Pack light. You'll walk with your luggage more than you think. Bring a single carry-on bag and a daypack. Use the packing checklist later in this book as a guide.

Amsterdam City Walk

From Centraal Station to Leidseplein

Take a Dutch sampler walk from one end of the old center to the other, tasting all that Amsterdam has to offer along the way. It's your best single stroll through quintessentially Dutch scenes, hidden churches, surprising shops, thriving happy-hour hangouts, and eight centuries of history.

The walk starts at Centraal Station, heads down touristy Damrak to Dam Square, and continues south down pedestrian-only Kalverstraat to the Mint Tower. Then it wafts through the flower market, before continuing south to busy Leidseplein. To return to Centraal Station, catch tram #2, #11, or #12 from Leidseplein.

ORIENTATION

Length of This Walk: About three miles—allow three hours.

When to Go: Best during the day, when sights are open.

Alert: Beware of silent transport—trams and bikes. Walkers should stay off the tram tracks and bike paths, and yield to bell-ringing bikers.

Royal Palace: €10, daily 10:00-17:00 but often closed for official business.

New Church: Free to view from gift-shop balcony, €9-16 to enter interior (depending on special exhibits), daily 10:00-17:00.

De Papegaai Hidden Church: Free, Mon-Sat 10:00-16:00, Sun until 14:00.

Amsterdam Museum: €15, daily 10:00-17:00.

Amsterdam Gallery: Free, daily 10:00-17:00.

Begijnhof: Free, daily 8:00-17:30.

Tours: 🎧 Download my free Amsterdam City Walk audio tour.

Services: You can find WCs at fast-food places, near the entrance to the Amsterdam Museum, and in the Kalvertoren shopping mall.

THE WALK BEGINS

❶ Centraal Station

Here, where today's train travelers enter the city, sailors of yore disembarked from seagoing ships. They were met by street musicians, pickpockets, hotel runners, and ladies carrying red lanterns. Centraal Station, built in the late 1800s, sits on reclaimed land at what was once the harbor mouth. With warm red brick and prickly spires, the station is the first of several Neo-Gothic buildings we'll see from the late 19th century, the era of Amsterdam's economic revival. One of the station's towers has a clock dial; the other tower's dial is a weather vane. Watch the hand twitch as the wind gusts in every direction—N, Z, O, and W.

Let's get oriented: *nord, zuid, ost,* and *vest.* Facing the station, you're facing north. Farther north, on the other side of the station, is the IJ (pronounced "eye"), the body of water that gives Amsterdam access to the open sea.

Now turn your back to the station and face the city, looking south. The city spreads out before you like a fan, in a series of concentric canals. Ahead of you stretches the street called Damrak, which leads—like a red carpet for guests entering Amsterdam—to Dam Square a half-mile away. That's where we're headed.

To the left of Damrak is the city's old (*oude*) town. The crown-topped steeple of the Old Church (Oude Kerk) marks its center. More recently, that historic quarter has become the Red Light District (□ see the Red Light District Walk). Closer to you, towering above the old part of town, is the domed St. Nicholas Church. It was built in the 1880s, when Catholics—after about three centuries of oppression—were finally free to worship in public. To your far left is the DoubleTree by Hilton Hotel, with its 11th-floor Sky Lounge Amsterdam offering perhaps the city's best viewpoint.

To the right of Damrak is the new (*nieuwe*) part of town, where you'll find the Anne Frank House and the peaceful Jordaan neighborhood.

The train station is the city's transportation center. Many trams and taxis leave from out front. Beneath your feet is a new Metro line. In the "Golden 1990s" when the economy was booming, Amsterdam committed the city to a grand infrastructure expansion to accommodate the tens of thousands of people living in North Amsterdam, the fast-growing suburb beyond the IJ. Today this plaza, while providing a people-friendly welcome to the city, also works as an efficient transit hub.

On your far right, in front of Ibis Hotel, is a huge, multistory **parking garage**—for bikes only. Biking in Holland is the way to go—the land is flat, distances are short, and there are designated bike paths everywhere. The bike parking garage is free, courtesy of the government, and intended to encourage this green and ultra-efficient mode of transportation.

Centraal Station, the city's transit hub

Bikes—and bike lanes—are everywhere.

> *Let's head out. With your back to the station, start walking south into the city to the head of Damrak. Be aware of trams and bikes as you cross the street. Keep going south straight along the right side of the street, following the crowds on...*

❷ Damrak

This street was once a riverbed. It's where the Amstel River flowed north into the IJ, which led to a vast inlet of the North Sea called the Zuiderzee. It's this unique geography that turned Amsterdam into a center of trade. Boats could sail up the Amstel into the interior of Europe, or out to the North Sea, to reach the rest of the world.

As you stroll along Damrak, look left. There's a marina, lined with old brick buildings. Though they aren't terribly historic, the scene still captures a bit of Golden Age Amsterdam. Think of it: Back in the 1600s, this area was the harbor, and those buildings warehoused exotic goods from all over the world.

All along Damrak, you'll pass a gauntlet of touristy shops. These seem to cover every Dutch cliché. You'll see wooden shoes, which the Dutch used to wear to get around easily in the marshy soil, and all manner of tulips; the real ones come from Holland's famed fresh-flower industry. Heineken fridge magnets advertise one of the world's most popular pilsner beers. There are wheels of cheese, marijuana-leaf hats, team jerseys for the Ajax football (soccer) club, and memorabilia with the city's "XXX" logo. You'll likely hear a hand-cranked barrel organ and see windmill-shaped saltshakers. And everything seems to be available in bright orange—the official color of the Dutch royal family.

At the **Damrak Sex Museum** at Damrak 18, you'll find the city's most notorious commodity on display. As a port town catering to sailors and businessmen away from home, Amsterdam has always accommodated the sex trade. Continue up Damrak. You'll pass places selling the popular local fast food: French fries. Here they're called ***Vlaamse friets***—Flemish fries—since they were invented in the Low Countries. The stand at Damrak 41 is a favorite, where plenty of locals stop to dip their fries in mayonnaise (not ketchup).

Farther up Damrak, you'll pass many restaurants. It quickly becomes obvious that, here, international cuisine is almost like going local. Restaurants serving **rijsttafel,** a sampler of assorted Indonesian dishes, are especially popular, thanks to the days when the Dutch

East Indies were a colony. Amsterdammers on the go usually just grab a simple sandwich *(broodje)* or a pita-bread wrap *(shoarma),* from a Middle Eastern takeout joint.

We're walking along what was once the Amstel River. Today, the Amstel is channeled into canals and its former mouth is covered by Centraal Station. But Amsterdam still remains a major seaport. That's because, in the 19th century, the Dutch dug the North Sea Canal to create a shorter route to the open sea. These days, more than 100,000 ships a year dock on the outskirts of Amsterdam, making it Europe's fourth-busiest seaport (giant cruise ships stop here as well). For all of Amsterdam's existence, it's been a trading center.

▶ *The long brick building with the square clock tower, along the left side of Damrak, is the...*

❸ Stock Exchange (Beurs van Berlage)

This impressive structure, a symbol of the city's long tradition as a trading town, was built with nine million bricks. Like so many buildings in this once-marshy city, it was constructed on a foundation of pilings—some 5,000 tree trunks hammered vertically into the soil. When the Beurs opened in 1903, it was one of the world's first modernist buildings, with a geometric, minimal, no-frills style. Emphasizing function over looks, it helped set the architectural tone for many 20th-century buildings.

Make your way to the end of the long, century-old building. Amsterdammers have gathered in this neighborhood to trade since medieval times. Back then, "trading stock" meant buying and selling goats, chickens, or kegs of beer. Over time, they began exchanging slips of paper, or "futures," rather than actual goods. Traders needed moneychangers, who needed bankers, who made money by lending money. By the 1600s, Amsterdam had become one of the world's first great capitalist cities, loaning money to free-spending kings, dukes, and bishops.

When you reach the end of the building, look (or detour) left into the square called **Beursplein.** In 1984, the Beurs building was turned into a cultural center, and the stock exchange moved next door to the Euronext complex. See the stock price readout board. How's your Heineken stock doing? Amsterdam still thrives as the center of Dutch business and, besides Heineken, is home to Shell Oil, Philips Electronics, and ING Bank. Directly opposite Beursplein on Damrak

Amsterdam City Walk

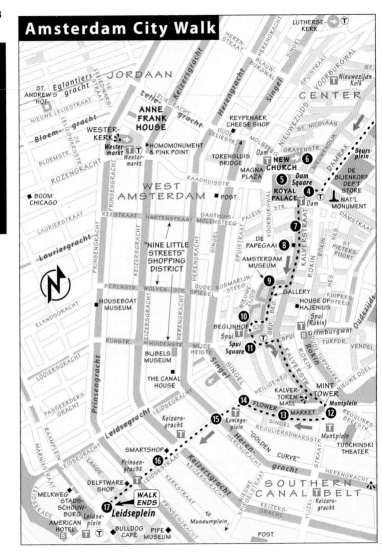

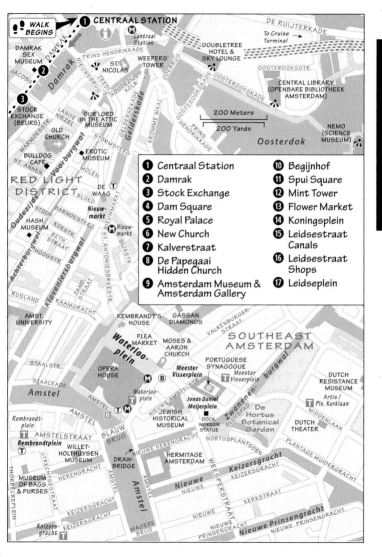

WALK BEGINS

1 CENTRAAL STATION

Centraal Station

DE RUIJTERKADE

To Cruise Terminal →

DOUBLETREE HOTEL & SKY LOUNGE

PRINS HENDRIKKADE

OOSTERDOKSSTR.

WEEPERS' TOWER

OOSTERDOKSKADE OOSTERDOK

CENTRAL LIBRARY (OPENBARE BIBLIOTHEEK AMSTERDAM)

DAMRAK SEX MUSEUM

ST. NICOLAS

OLEBERG

ZEEDIJK

OUDEZIJDS KOLK

NIEUWEBRUG

PRINS HENDRIKKADE

200 Meters
200 Yards

Oosterdok

NEMO (SCIENCE MUSEUM)

STOCK EXCHANGE (BEURS)

LANGE NIEZEL

OUR LORD IN THE ATTIC MUSEUM

GELDERSEKADE

KROMME WAAL

OOSTERDOKSKADE

WARMOESSTR.

OLD CHURCH

STORMSTEEG

BULLDOG CAFÉ

ST. ANNEN

EROTIC MUSEUM

MOLEN.

Voorburgwal

RED LIGHT DISTRICT

BLOED

DE WAAG

Nieuwmarkt

Oudezijds

STOOF

BARNDESTEEG

HASH MUSEUM

BETH. STRAAT

KOESTR.

HOOGSTR.

Achterburgwal

Nieuwmarkt

ST ANTONIESBREESTR.

DIJKSTR.

RUSLAND

Kloveniersburgwal

ZAND STRAAT

RAAMGRACHT

AMST. UNIVERSITY

REMBRANDT'S HOUSE

GASSAN DIAMONDS

VALKENBURGERSTRAAT

Waterlooplein

FLEA MARKET

MOSES & AARON CHURCH

SOUTHEAST AMSTERDAM

STAALSTR.

OPERA HOUSE

PORTUGUESE SYNAGOGUE

Meester Visserplein

Meester Visserplein

Nieuwe Amstel

burgwal

DUTCH RESISTANCE MUSEUM

STAALKADE

Amstel

Waterlooplein

Jonas Daniel Meijerplein

JEWISH HISTORICAL MUSEUM

Zwanenburgwal

SLUISPAD

De Hortus Botanical Garden

Artis / Pln. Kerklaan

MIDDENLAAN

AMSTEL

DOCK WORKER STATUE

DUTCH THEATER

Rembrandtplein

AMSTELSTRAAT

BLAUW BRUG

HORTUSPLANTSOEN

WEESPERSTRAAT

PLANTAGE MUIDERGRACHT

Rembrandtplein

WILLET-HOLTHUYSEN MUSEUM

UTRECHTSESTRAAT

Nieuwe Herengracht

HERMITAGE AMSTERDAM

Keizersgracht

MUSEUM OF BAGS & PURSES

DRAW-BRIDGE

HERENGRACHT

Nieuwe

KEIZERSGRACHT

KERKSTRAAT

THORBECKEPLEIN

Amstel

KEIZERSGRACHT

NIEUWE

NIEUWE

KEIZERSGRACHT

Keizersgracht

MAGERE BRUG

NIEUWE PRINSENGRACHT

Nieuwe Prinsengracht

NIEUWE PRINSENGRACHT

1 Centraal Station
2 Damrak
3 Stock Exchange
4 Dam Square
5 Royal Palace
6 New Church
7 Kalverstraat
8 De Papegaai Hidden Church
9 Amsterdam Museum & Amsterdam Gallery
10 Begijnhof
11 Spui Square
12 Mint Tower
13 Flower Market
14 Koningsplein
15 Leidsestraat Canals
16 Leidsestraat Shops
17 Leidseplein

is a fancy, faux Art Nouveau shopping passageway. You'll see chandeliers and Tiffany lanterns, a marble floor and mosaic ceiling, and fun Amsterdam imagery.

▶ *Continue up Damrak until it opens into Dam Square. Make your way—carefully—across the street to the cobblestone pavement. Now, stand in the middle of the square and take it all in.*

❹ Dam Square

This is the historic heart of Amsterdam. The city got its start right here in about the year 1250, when fishermen in this marshy delta settled along the built-up banks of the Amstel River. They built a *damme,* blocking the Amstel River, and creating a small village called "Amsteldamme." To the north was the *damrak* ("outer harbor"), a waterway that led to the sea. That's the street we just walked. To the south was the *rokin* ("inner harbor"), for river traffic. Fishermen were soon trading with German riverboats traveling downstream and with seafaring boats from Stockholm, Hamburg, and London. Dam Square was the center of it all.

Today, Dam Square is still the center of Dutch life, at least symbolically. The Royal Palace and major department stores face the square. Mimes, jugglers, and human statues mingle with locals and tourists. As Holland's most recognizable place, Dam Square is where political demonstrations begin and end.

Circling the Square: Pan the square clockwise, and take in the sights, starting with the Royal Palace—the large domed building on the west side. To its right stands the New Church (Nieuwe Kerk). Panning past Damrak, see the proud old De Bijenkorf ("The Beehive") department store (with a view café).

Farther right, the Grand Hotel Krasnapolsky has a lovely circa-1900 glass-roofed "winter garden." The white obelisk is the National Monument, built in 1956 to honor WWII casualties. When the Nazis occupied Holland from 1940 to 1945, they deported some 60,000 Jewish Amsterdammers, driving many—including young Anne Frank and her family—into hiding. The "Hunger Winter" of 1944-1945 killed thousands of Dutch and forced many to survive on little more than tulip bulbs. This obelisk—with its carvings of the crucified Christ, men in chains, and howling dogs—remembers the suffering of that grim time and is also considered a monument for peace. A few blocks behind the hotel is the edge of the Red Light District. To

Dam Square, with its WWII memorial, is the symbolic center of the Netherlands.

the right of the hotel stretches the street called the Nes, lined with some of Amsterdam's edgy live-theater venues. Panning farther right, find Rokin street—Damrak's southern counterpart. Next, just to the right of the touristy Madame Tussauds, is Kalverstraat, a busy pedestrian-only shoppers mall.

❺ Royal Palace (Koninklijk Huis)

Despite the name, this is really the former City Hall—and Amsterdam is one of the cradles of modern democracy. In medieval times, this was where the city council and mayor met. Amsterdam was a self-governing community that prided itself on its independence and thumbed its nose at royalty. In about 1650, the old medieval Town Hall was replaced with this one. Its style is appropriately Classical, recalling the democratic Greeks. The triangular pediment features denizens of the sea cavorting with Neptune and his gilded copper trident—all appropriate imagery for sea-trading Amsterdam. The small balcony (just above the entry doors) is where city leaders have long appeared for major speeches, pronouncements, executions, and (these days) for newly married royalty to blow kisses to the crowds.

Today, the palace remains one of the four official residences of King Willem-Alexander and is usually open to visitors (see page 128).

Amsterdam's Story

Beginnings: Situated at the mouth of the Amstel River, Amsterdam was where Rhine riverboats met sea-going vessels—trade flourished.

Around 1250, locals built a dam on the Amstel, creating "Amsteldam." They drained the marshy delta, channeled the water into canals, sank pilings, and built a city from scratch.

1300s Charter: Amsterdam was already an international trade center for German beer, locally caught herring, cloth, bacon, salt, and wine. When the region's leading bishop granted the town a charter (1300), Amsterdammers could then set up law courts, judge their own matters, and be essentially autonomous.

1500s Growth: Amsterdam became a bustling trade and banking center of 12,000 people crammed within the Singel canal. The walled city was ruled from afar by Catholic Habsburgs in Spain. Angry Protestants rose up, vandalizing Catholic churches and starting a war of independence (officially granted in 1648).

1600s Golden Age: Meanwhile, Holland was inventing the global economy. In 1602, hardy Dutch sailors (and Henry Hudson, an Englishman in Dutch service) tried their hand at trade with the Far East.

When they returned, they brought with them valuable spices, diamonds, rijsttafel recipes... and the Golden Age. The Dutch East India Company (abbreviated "VOC" in Dutch), a state-subsidized import/export business, combined nautical skills with capitalist investing. With 500 or so 150-foot ships cruising in and out of Amsterdam's harbor, it was the first great multinational corporation.

Golden Age Amsterdam (pop. 100,000) was perhaps the wealthiest city on earth—the "warehouse of the world." Goods came from everywhere. The VOC's specialties were spices (pepper and cinnamon), coffee and tea, Chinese porcelain, and silk. Meanwhile, the competing Dutch West India Company concentrated on the New World, trading African slaves for South American sugar. With its wealth, the city expanded west and south, adding new canals lined with gabled mansions. Rembrandt, Vermeer, and Hals captured the can-do spirit on canvas.

At the peak of the Golden Age, Amsterdam was gripped by "Tulip Mania." Investors drove the value of tulip bulbs to insane heights. Then in 1637, the market crashed, symbolically marking the end of the Golden Age. Soon, Holland was eclipsed by new superpowers England and France, who took over the overseas trade and scuttled their fleet in demoralizing wars.

1700s Decline: Amsterdam became a city of backwater bankers and small manufacturers—still a cultural center but befitting Holland's small size. The city hit rock bottom in 1795: French troops invaded, and proud Holland was soon saddled with a monarchy.

1800s Revival: The tech-minded Dutch built a canal to the North Sea, rejuvenating Amsterdam's port. Railroads laced the country, and Amsterdam expanded southward by draining new land. The Rijksmuseum, Centraal Station, and Magna Plaza (formerly the main post office) date from this economic upswing.

1900s: The 1930s Depression hit hard, followed by five years of occupation under the Nazis, aided by pro-Nazi Dutch. The city's large Jewish population was decimated by Nazi deportations and extermination (falling from about 75,000 Jews in 1940 to just 15,000 in 1945). With postwar prosperity, 1960s Amsterdam became a global center for Europe's hippies, promoting legal marijuana, free sex, and free bikes.

Today: Amsterdam is now a city of 820,000 people jammed into small apartments (often with the same floor plan as their neighbors). Since the 1970s, many immigrants have become locals. One in 10 Amsterdammers is Surinamese, and one in 10 prays toward Mecca.

City on a Sandbar

Amsterdam sits in the marshy delta at the mouth of the Amstel River—a completely man-made city, built on millions of wooden pilings. (The wood survives if kept wet and out of the air.)

Since World War II, concrete has been used for the pilings, with foundations driven 60 feet deep through a layer of sand, then mud, and into a second layer of sand. Today's biggest buildings have foundations that go down as far as 120 feet. Yet, many of the city's buildings tend to lean this way and that as their pilings settle.

▶ *A few paces away, to the right as you're facing the Royal Palace, is the...*

❻ New Church (Nieuwe Kerk)

Though called the "New" Church, this building is actually 600 years old—a mere 100 years newer than the "Old" Church (in the Red Light District). The sundial above the entrance once served as the city's official timepiece.

While it's pricey to enter the church, cheapskates can actually see much of it for free. Enter the gift shop (through the "Museumshop" door to the left of the main entrance) and climb the stairs to a balcony with a small free museum and great views of the nave.

The church's bare, spacious, well-lit interior (occupied by a new art exhibit every three months) looks quite different from the Baroque-encrusted churches found in the rest of Europe. In 1566, clear-eyed Protestant extremists throughout Holland marched into Catholic churches (including this one), lopped off the heads of holy statues, stripped gold-leaf angels from the walls, urinated on Virgin Marys, and shattered stained-glass windows in a wave of anti-Catholic vandalism.

This iconoclasm (icon-breaking) of 1566 started an 80-year war against Spain and the Habsburgs, leading finally to Dutch independence in 1648. Catholic churches like this one were converted to the new dominant religion, Calvinist Protestantism (today's Dutch Reformed Church). From then on, Dutch churches downplayed the "graven images" and "idols" of ornate religious art.

Take in the church's main highlights. At the far left end is an organ from 1655, still played for midday concerts. Opposite the entrance,

Royal Palace on Dam Square New Church, where monarchs are crowned

a stained-glass window shows Count William IV giving the city its "XXX" coat of arms. And the window over the entrance portrays the inauguration of Queen Wilhelmina (1880-1962), who became the steadfast center of the Dutch resistance during World War II. The choir, once used by the monks, was turned into a mausoleum for a great Dutch admiral after the Reformation.

This church is where many of the Netherlands' monarchs are married, and all are "inaugurated." Imagine the church in action in April 2013, when King Willem-Alexander—Wilhelmina's great-grandson—was paraded through this church to the golden choir screen. The king, wearing a tuxedo with an orange sash, is presented with the royal crown, scepter, orb, sword, and a copy of the Dutch constitution. With TV lights glaring and cameras flashing, he is sworn in as the new sovereign.

▶ *From Dam Square, head south (at the Rabobank sign) on...*

❼ Kalverstraat

Kalverstraat (strictly pedestrian-only—even bikers need to dismount and walk) has been a traditional shopping street for centuries. But today it's notorious among locals as a noisy, soulless string of chain stores. For smaller and more elegant stores, try the adjacent district called De Negen Straatjes ("The Nine Little Streets"). Only about four blocks west of Kalverstraat, it's where 200 or so shops and cafés mingle along tranquil canals.

▶ *About 100 yards along, keep a sharp eye out for the next sight (it's fairly easy to miss): on the right, just before and across from the Mc-Donald's, at #58. Now pop into...*

❽ De Papegaai Hidden Church (Petrus en Paulus Kerk)

This Catholic church is an oasis of peace amid crass 21st-century commercialism. It's not exactly a hidden church (after all, you've found it), but it still keeps a low profile. That's because it dates from an era when Catholics in Amsterdam were forced to worship in secret.

In the 1500s, Protestants were fighting Catholics all over Europe. For the next two centuries, Amsterdam's Catholics were driven underground. While technically illegal here, Catholicism was tolerated. Catholics could worship so long as they practiced in humble, unadvertised places, like this church.

The church gets its nickname from a parrot (*papegaai*) carved over the entrance of the house that formerly stood on this site. Now, a stuffed parrot hangs in the nave to remember that original *papegaai*.

▶ *Return to Kalverstraat and continue south for about 100 yards. At #92, where Kalverstraat crosses Wijde Kapel Steeg, look to the right at an archway that leads to the...*

❾ Amsterdam Museum and Amsterdam Gallery

Pause at the entrance to the museum complex to view the archway with Amsterdam's coat of arms. The X-shaped crosses on the red shield represent (not the sex trade, but...) the crucifixion of St. Andrew, the patron saint of fishermen. The crown is the Habsburg royal crown, granted to Amsterdam as thanks for a loan from Dutch bankers.

Continue under the arch, past a pleasant café, a shaded courtyard, and lockers from the old orphanage. Up ahead is the **Amsterdam Museum** (described on page 130).

Next to the museum's entrance is a free, glassed-in passageway lined with paintings. If it's closed, you'll need to backtrack to Kalverstraat to continue our walk (continue south, then turn right on Begijnensteeg, then look for the gate leading to the Begijnhof). Otherwise, step into the **Amsterdam Gallery** (formerly known as the "Civic Guards Gallery").

This hall features group portraits of Amsterdam's citizens from the Golden Age to modern times. Giant statues of Goliath and a knee-high David (from 1650) watch over the whole thing.

Stroll around and gaze into the eyes of the hardworking men and women who made tiny Holland so prosperous and powerful. These are ordinary middle-class people, merchants, and traders, dressed in their Sunday best. They come across as good people—honest, businesslike, and friendly.

The Dutch got rich the old-fashioned way—they earned it. By 1600, Holland's merchant fleets commanded the seas. Traders, who were financed by shrewd Amsterdam businessmen, flourished by shipping goods from Dutch colonies as far away as India, the East Indies, and America.

The portraits show the men gathered with their Civic Guard militia units. These men defended Holland, but the Civic Guards were also fraternal organizations of business bigwigs—the Rotary Clubs of the 17th century. The weapons they carry—pikes and muskets—are mostly symbolic.

Many paintings look the same in this highly stylized genre. The men usually sit arranged in two rows. Someone holds the militia's flag. Later group portraits showed "captains" of industry going about their work, dressed in suits, along with the tools of their trade—ledger books, quill pens, and money.

Everyone looks straight out, and every face is lit perfectly. Each paid for his own portrait and wanted it right. It took masters like Rembrandt and Frans Hals to take the starch out of the collars and compose more natural scenes.

Now focus on some more modern portraits. You may see simple photos of today's ordinary citizens—workers, police—the backbone of this democracy, or the modern-day town council posing playfully as Golden Age bigwigs.

▶ *Exit out the far end of the gallery. Once in the light of day, continue ahead one block farther south and find the humble gate on the right, which leads to the...*

The Amsterdam Museum's entrance arch

Civic Guard group portrait—"Say *kaas*."

⑩ Begijnhof

This quiet courtyard, lined with houses around a church, has sheltered women since 1346. For centuries this was the home of a community of Beguines—pious and simple women who removed themselves from the world at large to dedicate their lives to God.

As you enter, keep in mind that this spot isn't just a tourist attraction; it's also a place where people live. Be considerate: Don't photograph the residents or their homes, be quiet, and stick to the area near the churches.

Begin your visit just beyond the church at the **statue** of one of these charitable sisters. The Beguines' ranks swelled during the Crusades, when so many men took off, never to return. Later, women widowed by the hazards of overseas trade lived out their days as Beguines. Poor and rich women alike turned their backs on materialism and marriage to live here in Christian poverty. They spent their days deep in prayer and busy with daily tasks—spinning wool, making lace, teaching, and caring for the sick.

Now turn your attention to the brick-faced **English Reformed church** (Engelse Kerk), built in 1420 to serve the Beguine community. In 1607, this church became Anglican. It served as a refuge for English traders and religious separatists fleeing persecution in England. Strict Protestants such as the famous Pilgrims found sanctuary in tolerant Amsterdam and may have worshipped in this church.

If the church is open, step inside, and head to the far end, toward the stained-glass window. It shows the Pilgrims praying before boarding the Mayflower. Along the right-hand wall is an old pew (with columns and clock) they may have sat on, and on the altar is a Bible from 1763, with lotſ of old-ſtyle ſ 's. Also of note is the front pulpit, carved

Begijnhof—quiet courtyard for lay sisters

Beautiful interior of the "hidden" Catholic church

of wood. It's by Piet Mondrian, the famous Dutch abstract artist, and was one of his first professional gigs.

Back outside, find the **Catholic church,** which faces the English Reformed Church. Because Catholics were being persecuted when it was built, this had to be a low-profile, "hidden" church—notice the painted-out windows on the second and third floors. Step inside, through the low-profile doorway. It's decorated lovingly, if on the cheap (try tapping softly on a "marble" column). Amsterdam's Catholics must have eagerly awaited the day when they were legally allowed to say Mass (that day finally came in the 19th century).

Today, Holland still has something of a religious divide, but not a bitter one. Amsterdam itself is pretty un-churched. But the Dutch countryside is much more religious, including a "Bible Belt" region where 98 percent of the population is Protestant. Overall, in the Netherlands, the country is divided fairly evenly between Catholics, Protestants, and those who see Sunday as a day to sleep in and enjoy a lazy brunch.

Step back outside. The last Beguine died in 1971, but this Begijnhof still thrives, providing subsidized housing to about 100 single women (mostly Catholic seniors). The Begijnhof is just one of a few dozen *hofjes* (little housing projects surrounding courtyards) that dot Amsterdam.

The statue of the Beguine faces a black **wooden house,** at #34, and is the city's oldest. Originally, the whole city consisted of wooden houses like this one. They were eventually replaced with brick houses to minimize the fire danger.

▶ *Near the wooden house and gables, find a little corridor leading you back into the modern world. Head up the six steps to emerge into the lively...*

⓫ Spui Square

Lined with cafés and bars, this square is one of the city's more popular spots for nightlife and sunny afternoon people-watching. Its name, Spui (rhymes with "now" and means "spew"), recalls the days when water was moved over dikes to keep the place dry.

Head two blocks to the left, crossing busy Kalverstraat, to the street called the Rokin. Turn left and walk up 50 yards to a mecca for cigar connoisseurs—the **House of Hajenius** cigar store, at Rokin 92.

Enter this sumptuous Art Deco building with painted leather ceilings. Don't be shy—the place is as much a free museum for visitors as it is a store for paying customers.

From Hajenius, backtrack to Kalverstraat and continue south. Just before the end of this shopping boulevard, on the right, you'll see modern **Kalvertoren** shopping mall. Enter and find a slanting glass elevator. You can ride this to the recommended top-floor **Blue Amsterdam Restaurant,** where a coffee or light lunch buys you something that's rare in altitude-challenged Amsterdam—a nice view.

▸ *At the center of the square stands the...*

⓬ Mint Tower (Munttoren)

This tower marked the limit of the medieval walled city and served as one of its original gates. In the Middle Ages, the city walls were girdled by a moat—the Singel canal. Until about 1500, the area beyond here was nothing but marshy fields and a few farms on reclaimed land. The Mint Tower's steeple was added later—in the year 1620, as you can see written below the clock face.

Today, the tower is a favorite within Amsterdam's marijuana culture. Stoners love to take a photo of the clock and its 1620 sign at exactly 4:20 p.m.—the traditional time to quit work and light one up. (On the 24-hour clock, 4:20 p.m. is 16:20...Du-u-u-ude!)

▸ *Continue past the Mint Tower, first walking a few yards south along busy Vijzelstraat (keep an eye out for trams). Then turn right and walk west along the south bank of the Singel canal. It's lined with the greenhouse shops of the...*

⓭ Flower Market (Bloemenmarkt)

The stands along this busy block sell cut flowers, plants, bulbs, seeds, garden supplies, and flower-oriented souvenirs and knickknacks. Browse your way along while heading for the end of the block.

The Flower Market is a testament to Holland's long-time love affair with flowers. The Netherlands is by far the largest flower exporter in Europe, and a major flower power worldwide. If you're looking for a souvenir, note that certain seeds are marked as OK to bring back through customs into the US (the marijuana starter-kit-in-a-can is probably...not).

The best-known Dutch flower, the tulip, was brought from

The Mint Tower once marked the border of the medieval, walled city.

"Tulip mania" lives on at the Flower Market.

Be daring—try a herring.

central Asia in the mid-1500s. The hardy bulbs thrived in the sandy soil of Holland's reclaimed land. Within a generation, tulips grew from a trendy fad into an all-out frenzy. Soon, a single prized bulb could sell for the equivalent of thousands of dollars. By 1636, it was full-blown "Tulip mania"—yes, that's what even the Dutch called it. Then in 1637 the tulip bubble burst. Overnight, once-wealthy investors were broke. The crash was devastating, even playing a role in the decline of the Golden Age. But Holland's love of this delightful flower lived on. Today, tulips are a major export, and are firmly planted in the Dutch psyche.

▶ *The long Flower Market ends at the next bridge, where you'll see a square named...*

⓮ Koningsplein

This pleasant square, with a popular outdoor herring shop, is a great place to choke down a raw herring. The sign—*Hollandse nieuwe*—means the herring are "new" (fresh), caught during the May-June season. Locals eat it chopped up with onions and pickles, using the Dutch-flag toothpick as a utensil. Elsewhere in the Netherlands, people tend to eat the fish whole—grab it by the tail, tip your head back, and down she goes.

▶ *Turn left, heading straight south to Leidseplein along Koningsplein, which changes its name to Leidsestraat.*

⓯ Leidsestraat Canals and ⓰ Shops

As you walk along, you'll reach Herengracht, the first of several grand canals. Look left down Herengracht to see the so-called **Golden Curve** of the canal. It's lined with townhouses sporting especially

Leidsestraat—busy with shoppers (and trams)   Delftware—blue-painted ceramics

nice gables. Amsterdam has many different types of gable—bell-shaped, step-shaped, and so on. This stretch is best known for its "cornice" gables (straight across); these topped the Classical-looking facades belonging to rich merchants—the *heren*. (For more on gables, see the sidebar on page 95.)

There are so many canals in Amsterdam because the city was founded in a marshy river delta, so they needed to keep the water at bay. They dammed the Amstel River and channeled it safely away into canals, creating pockets of dry land to build on.

The word *gracht* (pronounced, roughly, "hroht," with guttural flair) can refer to a canal itself, or to the ensemble of a canal and the lanes that border it. Today, the city has about 100 canals, most of which are about 10 feet deep. They're crossed by some 1,200 bridges, fringed with 100,000 Dutch elm and lime trees, and bedecked with 2,500 houseboats. A system of locks (near Centraal Station) controls the flow and are opened periodically to flush out the system.

After the bridge, Koningsplein becomes Leidsestraat. It's a busy street, crowded with shoppers, tourists, bicycles, and trams (don't walk on the tram tracks). Notice that, as the street narrows, trams must wait their turn to share a single track.

Cross over the next canal (Keizersgracht) and find the little **smartshop** on the right-hand corner (at Keisersgracht 508). While "smartshops" like this one are all just as above-board as any other in the city, they sell drugs—some of them quite strong, most of them illegal back home, and not all of them harmless. But since all these products are found in nature, the Dutch government considers them legal. You can check out the window displays, or go on in and browse.

Just over the next bridge, where Leidsestraat crosses Prin-

The Bulldog Café coffeeshop on Leidseplein is a good place to kick back after this walk.

sengracht, you'll find a **Delftware shop** (to the right, at Prinsengracht 440). This place sells good examples of the glazed ceramics known as Delftware, famous for its distinctive blue-and-white designs. In the early 1600s, Dutch traders brought home blue-and-white porcelain from China, which became so popular that Dutch potters scrambled to come up with their own version. It was traditionally made in Delft, the quaint town about 30 miles southwest of here. You might spot a tulip vase in the window: a tall, tapering "flower pagoda" with multiple spouts for displaying the prized flower.

▶ *Follow Leidsestraat down to the big, busy square, called...*

⑰ Leidseplein

This is Amsterdam's liveliest square: filled with outdoor tables under trees; ringed with cafés, theaters, and nightclubs; bustling with tourists, diners, trams, mimes, and fire eaters. No wonder locals and tourists alike come here day and night to sit under the trees and sip a coffee or beer in the warmth of the sun or the glow of lantern light.

Do a 360-degree spin: Leidseplein's south side is bordered by a gray Neoclassical building that houses a huge Apple Store—sitting on what may be the city's most expensive piece of real estate. Nearby is the city's main serious theater, the **Stadsschouwburg.**

To the right of the Stadsschouwburg, down a lane behind the big theater, you'll find the **Melkweg** ("Milky Way") nightclub. Back in the 1970s, this place was almost mythical—an entertainment complex entirely devoted to the young generation and their desires.

Continue panning. The neighborhood beyond Burger King is Amsterdam's **"Restaurant Row,"** featuring countless Thai, Brazilian, Indian, Italian, Indonesian—and even a few Dutch—eateries.

Next, on the east end of Leidseplein, is the flagship **Bulldog Café coffeeshop.** (Notice the sign above the door: It once housed the police bureau.) A small green-and-white decal on the window indicates that it's a city-licensed "coffeeshop," where marijuana is sold and smoked legally. Incredible as that may seem to visitors from many of the States, it's been going on here in Amsterdam for nearly four decades—another Dutch cliché alongside windmill peppermills and wooden shoes.

▶ *Our walk is over. But those with more energy could get out their maps and make their way to Vondelpark or the Rijksmuseum (one stop away on tram #2 or #12). To return to Centraal Station (or to nearly any place along this walk), catch tram #2, #11, or #12 from Leidseplein.*

Rijksmuseum Tour

At Amsterdam's Rijksmuseum ("Rijks" rhymes with "bikes"), Holland's Golden Age shines with the best collection anywhere of the Dutch Masters—from Vermeer's quiet domestic scenes and Steen's raucous family meals to Hals' snapshot portraits and Rembrandt's moody brilliance.

The 17th century saw the Netherlands at the pinnacle of its power. Trade and shipping boomed, wealth poured in, and the arts flourished. Upper-middle-class businessmen hired artists to paint their portraits and decorate their homes with pretty still lifes and unpreachy, slice-of-life art.

Dutch art is meant to be enjoyed, not studied. It's straightforward, meat-and-potatoes art for the common man. On this visit, we'll enjoy the beauty of everyday things rendered in exquisite detail. Set your cerebral cortex on "low" and let this art pass straight from the eyes to the heart, with minimal detours.

ORIENTATION

Cost: €17.50, covered by Museumkaart and I Amsterdam City Card.

Hours: Daily 9:00-17:00.

Information: Tel. 020/674-7047, www.rijksmuseum.nl.

Advance Tickets: Buy tickets online at www.rijksmuseum.nl (good any time) and you can enter the building through a less-crowded entrance, skip the ticket-buying lines, and go directly to the ticket taker.

Avoiding Crowds/Lines: The museum is most crowded on weekends and holidays, and between 11:00 and 14:00. It's least crowded after 15:00.

Getting There: From Centraal Station, catch tram #2 or #12 to the Rijksmuseum stop. The museum entrance is inside the arched passage that cuts under the building at its center.

Tours: The museum's free app offers tours, maps, and useful info (download in advance or use the museum's free Wi-Fi). Guided tours are often offered at 11:00, 13:00, and 15:00 (€5). A multimedia videoguide (€5) provides a 45-minute highlights tour and an in-depth version.

Length of This Tour: Allow 1.5 hours.

Services: The helpful info desk in the lower-level Atrium has free maps and baggage check.

Cuisine Art: The Rijksmuseum Café is in the Atrium. (No museum ticket required to eat here.) Beyond the museum complex, you'll find the Cobra Café on Museumplein. Vondelpark and Museumplein are perfect for picnics.

Starring: Rembrandt van Rijn, Frans Hals, Johannes Vermeer, Jan Steen.

The Rijksmuseum, on pleasant Museumplein

The Atrium has tourist services.

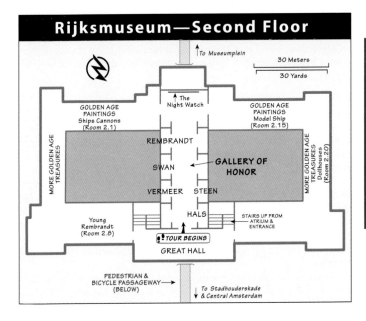

Rijksmuseum—Second Floor

↑ To Museumplein

30 Meters

30 Yards

GOLDEN AGE
PAINTINGS
Ships Cannons
(Room 2.1)

GOLDEN AGE
PAINTINGS
Model Ship
(Room 2.15)

↑ The
Night Watch

MORE GOLDEN AGE TREASURES

MORE GOLDEN AGE TREASURES
Dollhouses
(Room 2.20)

REMBRANDT

SWAN

GALLERY OF HONOR

VERMEER   STEEN

HALS

Young
Rembrandt
(Room 2.8)

STAIRS UP FROM
ATRIUM &
ENTRANCE

⚠ TOUR BEGINS

GREAT HALL

PEDESTRIAN &
BICYCLE PASSAGEWAY →
(BELOW)

↓ To Stadhouderskade
& Central Amsterdam

THE TOUR BEGINS

▶ *Descend into the lower-level Atrium. Show your ticket (and download the museum app or rent a videoguide), then follow the crowds up the stairway to the top (second) floor, into the* **Great Hall.** *With its stained-glass windows, vaulted ceiling, and murals of Golden Age explorers, it feels like a cathedral to Holland's middle-class merchants. Now, follow the flow into the...*

Gallery of Honor

This grand space was purpose-built to hold the Greatest Hits of the Golden Age by the era's biggest rock stars: Hals, Vermeer, Steen, and Rembrandt. The best of the era's portraits, still lifes, landscapes, and slice-of-life "genre scenes" give us a close-up look at daily life in this happy, affluent era.

Frans Hals

Frans Hals (c. 1582-1666) was the premier Golden Age portrait paint-er. Merchants hired him the way we'd hire a wedding photographer. With a few quick strokes, Hals captured not only the features, but also the personality.

A Militiaman Holding a Berkemeyer, a.k.a. *The Merry Drinker,* c. 1628-1630

You're greeted by a jovial man in a black hat, capturing the earthy, ex-uberant spirit of the Dutch Golden Age. Notice the details—the happy red face of the man offering us a *berkemeyer* drinking glass, the spar-kle in his eyes, the lacy collar, the decorative belt buckle, and so on.

Now move in closer. All these meticulous details are accom-plished with a few thick, messy brushstrokes. The beard is a tangle of brown worms, the belt buckle a yellow blur. His hand is a study in smudges. Even the expressive face is created with a few well-chosen patches of color. Unlike Dutch still-life scenes, this canvas is meant to be viewed from a distance, where the colors and brushstrokes blend together.

Rather than posing his subject, making him stand for hours say-ing "cheese," Hals tried to catch him at a candid moment. He often painted common people, fishermen, and barflies such as this one. He had to work quickly to capture the serendipity of the moment. Hals used a stop-action technique, freezing the man in mid-gesture, with the rough brushwork creating a blur that suggests the man is still moving.

Two centuries later, the Impressionists learned from Hals' scruffy brushwork. In the Van Gogh Museum, you'll see how Van Gogh painted, say, a brown beard by using thick dabs of green, yellow, and red that blend at a distance to make brown.

Portrait of a Couple, Probably Isaac Abrahamsz Massa and Beatrix van der Laen, c. 1622

This likely wedding portrait of a chubby, pleasant merchant and his bride sums up the story of the Dutch Golden Age. Because this over-seas trader was away from home for years at a time on business, Hals makes a special effort to point out his patron's commitment to mar-riage. Isaac pledges allegiance to his wife, putting his hand on his heart. Beatrix's wedding ring is prominently displayed dead center

The Dutch Golden Age (1600s)

Who bought this art? Look around at the Rijksmuseum's many portraits, and you'll see ordinary middle-class people, merchants, and traders. Even in their Sunday best, you can tell that these are hardworking, businesslike, friendly, simple people (with a penchant for ruffled lace collars).

By 1600, Holland's merchant fleets ruled the waves with colonies as far away as India, the East Indies, and America (remember—New York was originally "New Amsterdam"). Back home, these traders were financed by shrewd Amsterdam businessmen on the new frontiers of capitalism.

Look around again. Is there even one crucifixion? One saint? One Madonna? In most countries, Catholic bishops and rich kings supported the arts. But the Dutch Republic was independent, democratic, and largely Protestant, with no taste for saints and Madonnas.

Instead, Dutch burghers bought portraits of themselves and pretty, unpreachy, unpretentious works for their homes—landscapes, portraits (often of groups), scenes from everyday life, and still lifes of food and mundane objects.

between them (on her right-hand forefinger, Protestant-style). The vine clinging to a tree is a symbol of man's support and woman's dependence. And in the distance at right, in the classical love garden, are other happy couples strolling arm-in-arm amid peacocks, a symbol of fertility.

In earlier times, marriage portraits put the man and wife in separate canvases, staring out grimly. Hals' jolly side-by-side couple reflects a societal shift from marriage as business partnership to an arrangement that's more friendly and intimate.

Hals didn't need symbolism to tell us that these two are prepared for their long-distance relationship—they seem relaxed together, but each looks at us directly, with a strong, individual identity. Good as gold, these are the type of people who propelled this soggy little country into its glorious Golden Age.

▶ *A little farther along are the small-scale canvases of...*

Johannes Vermeer

Vermeer (1632-1675) is the master of tranquility and stillness. He creates a clear and silent pool that is a world in itself. Most of his canvases show interiors of Dutch homes, where Dutch women engage in everyday activities, lit by a side window.

Vermeer's father, an art dealer, gave Johannes a passion for painting. Late in the artist's career, with Holland drained by wars against England, the demand for art and luxuries went sour, forcing Vermeer to downsize—he sold his big home, packed up his wife and 14 children, and moved in with his mother-in-law. He died two years later, and his works fell into centuries of obscurity.

The Rijksmuseum has the best collection of Vermeers in the world—four of them. (There are only some 34 in captivity.) But each is a small jewel worth lingering over.

The Milkmaid, c. 1660

It's so quiet you can practically hear the milk pouring into the bowl.

Vermeer brings out the beauty in everyday things. The subject is ordinary—a kitchen maid—but you could look for hours at the tiny details and rich color tones. These are everyday objects, but they glow in a diffused light: the crunchy crust, the hanging basket, even the rusty nail in the wall with its tiny shadow. Vermeer had a unique ability with surface texture, to show how things feel when you touch them.

The maid is alive with Vermeer's distinctive yellow and blue—the colors of many traditional Dutch homes—against a white backdrop.

Vermeer's *Milkmaid*—quiet beauty   *Woman Reading a Letter*—from whom?

She is content, solid, and sturdy, performing this simple task as if it's the most important thing in the world. Her full arms are built with patches of reflected light. Vermeer squares off a little world in itself (framed by the table in the foreground, the wall in back, the window to the left, and the footstool at right), then fills this space with objects for our perusal.

Woman Reading a Letter, c. 1663

Notice how Vermeer's placid scenes often have an air of mystery. The woman is reading a letter. From whom? A lover? A father on a two-year business trip to the East Indies? Not even taking time to sit down, she reads intently, with parted lips and a bowed head. It must be important. (She looks pregnant, adding to the mystery, but that may just be the cut of her clothes.)

Again, Vermeer has framed a moment of everyday life. But within this small world are hints of a wider, wilder world—the light coming from the left is obviously from a large window, giving us a whiff of the life going on outside. The map hangs prominently, reminding us of travel, and perhaps of where the letter is from.

The Love Letter, c. 1669-1670

There's a similar theme here. The curtain parts, and we see through the doorway into a dollhouse world, then through the seascape on the back wall to the wide ocean. A woman is playing a lute when she's interrupted by a servant bringing a letter. The mysterious letter stops the music, intruding like a pebble dropped into the pool of Vermeer's quiet world. The floor tiles create a strong 3-D perspective that sucks us straight into the center of the painting—the woman's heart.

Vermeer's *The Love Letter*   *View of Houses in Delft*—Vermeer's hometown

Shhh...Dutch Art

You're sitting at home late one night, and it's perfectly calm. Not a sound, very peaceful. And then...the refrigerator motor turns off, and it's really quiet.

Dutch art is really quiet art. It silences our busy world, so that every sound, every motion is noticeable. You can hear cows tearing off grass 50 yards away. We notice how the cold night air makes the stars sharp.

One of the museum's most exciting, dramatic, emotional, and extravagant Dutch paintings is probably *The Threatened Swan* (in the Gallery of Honor). It's quite a contrast to the rape scenes and visions of heaven of Italian Baroque paintings from the same time period.

View of Houses in Delft, a.k.a. *The Little Street*, c. 1658

Vermeer was born in the picturesque town of Delft, grew up near its Market Square, and set a number of his paintings there. This may be the view from his front door.

The details in the painting actually aren't very detailed—the cobblestone street doesn't have a single individual stone in it. But Vermeer shows us the beautiful interplay of colored rectangles on the buildings. Our eye moves back and forth from shutter to gable to window...and then from front to back, as we notice the woman deep in the alleyway.

▶ *In an alcove nearby are some rollicking paintings by...*

Jan Steen

Not everyone could afford a masterpiece, but even poorer people wanted works of art for their homes (like a landscape from Sears for over the sofa). Jan Steen (c. 1625-1679, pronounced "yahn stain"), the Norman Rockwell of his day, painted humorous scenes from the lives of the lower classes. As a tavern owner, he observed society firsthand.

The Feast of St. Nicholas, 1665-1668

It's Christmas time, and the kids have been given their gifts, including a little girl who got a doll. The mother says, "Let me see it," but the girl turns away playfully. Everyone is happy except the boy, who's crying. His Christmas present is only a branch in his shoe—like coal in your stocking, the gift for bad boys. His sister gloats and passes it around. The kids laugh at him. But wait—it turns out the family is just playing a trick. In the background, the grandmother beckons to him, saying, "Look, I have your real present in here." Out of the limelight, but smack in the middle, sits the father providing ballast to this family scene and clearly enjoying his children's pleasure.

Steen has frozen the moment, sliced off a piece, and laid it on a canvas. He's told a story with a past, a present, and a future. These are real people in a real scene.

Steen's fun art reminds us that museums aren't mausoleums.

Adolf and Catharina Croeser, a.k.a. The Burgomaster of Delft and His Daughter, 1655

Steen's well-dressed burgher sits on his front porch, when a poor woman and child approach to beg, putting him squarely between the horns of a moral dilemma. On the one hand, we see his rich home, well-dressed daughter, and a vase of flowers—a symbol that his money came from morally suspect capitalism (the kind that produced the folly of 1637's "tulip mania"). On the other hand, there are his poor fellow citizens and the church steeple, reminding him of his Christian duty. The man's daughter avoids the confrontation. Will the burgher set the right Christian example? This moral dilemma perplexed many nouveau-riche Dutch Calvinists of Steen's day.

This early painting by Steen demonstrates his mastery of several popular genres: portrait, still life (the flowers and fabrics), cityscape, and moral instruction.

The Merry Family, 1668

This family—three generations living happily under one roof—is eating, drinking, and singing like there's no tomorrow. The broken eggshells and scattered cookware symbolize waste and extravagance. The neglected

Steen—playful family scene at Christmas

Steen—a rich burgher's moral dilemma

Steen's *Merry Family* may not be morally upright, but they sure know how to have fun.

proverb tacked to the fireplace reminds us that children will follow in the footsteps of their parents. The father in this jolly scene is very drunk—ready to topple over—while in the foreground his mischievous daughter is feeding her brother wine straight from the flask. Mom and Grandma join the artist himself (playing the bagpipes) in a lively sing-along, but the child learning to smoke would rather follow Dad's lead.

Dutch Golden Age families were notoriously lenient with their kids. Even today, the Dutch describe a rowdy family as a "Jan Steen household."

Rembrandt van Rijn

Rembrandt van Rijn (1606-1669) is the greatest of all Dutch painters. Whereas most painters specialized in one field—portraits, landscapes, still lifes—Rembrandt excelled in them all.

The son of a Leiden miller who owned a waterwheel on the Rhine ("van Rijn"), Rembrandt took Amsterdam by storm with his famous painting *The Anatomy Lesson of Dr. Nicolaes Tulp* (1632, currently in The Hague). The commissions poured in for official portraits, and he

Ruffs

I cannot tell you why men and women of the Dutch Golden Age found these fanlike collars attractive, but they certainly were all the rage here and elsewhere in Europe. It started in Spain in the 1540s, but the style really took off with a marvelous discovery in 1565: starch. Within decades,

Europe's wealthy merchant class was wearing nine-inch collars made from 18 yards of material.

The ruffs were detachable and made from a long, pleated strip of linen set into a neck (or wrist) band. You tied it in front with strings. Big ones required that you wear a wire frame underneath for support. There were various types—the "cartwheel" was the biggest, a "double ruff" had two layers of pleats, and a "cabbage" was somewhat asymmetrical.

Ruffs required elaborate maintenance. First, you washed and starched the linen. While the cloth was still wet, hot metal pokers were painstakingly inserted into the folds to form the characteristic figure-eight pattern. The ruffs were stored in special round boxes to hold their shape.

For about a century, Europeans loved the ruff, but by 1630, Holland had come to its senses, and the fad faded.

was soon wealthy and married (1634) to Saskia van Uylenburgh. They moved to an expensive home in the Jewish Quarter (today's Rembrandt House Museum) and decorated it with their collection of art and exotic furniture. His portraits were dutifully detailed, but other paintings explored strong contrasts of light and dark, with dramatic composition.

In 1642, Saskia died, and Rembrandt's fortunes changed, as the public's taste shifted and commissions dried up. In 1649, he hired an 18-year-old model named Hendrickje Stoffels, and she soon moved in with him and gave birth to their daughter.

Holland's war with England (1652-1654) devastated the art market, and Rembrandt's free-spending ways forced him to declare bankruptcy (1656)—the ultimate humiliation in success-oriented Amsterdam. The commissions came more slowly. The money ran out. His mother died. He had to auction off his paintings and furniture to pay debts. He moved out of his fine house to a cheaper place on Rozengracht. His bitter losses added a new wisdom to his work.

In his last years, Rembrandt's greatest works were his self-portraits, showing a tired, wrinkled man stoically enduring life's misfortunes. Rembrandt piled on layers of paint and glaze to capture increasingly subtle effects. In 1668, his lone surviving son, Titus, died, and Rembrandt passed away the next year. His death effectively marked the end of the Dutch Golden Age.

Isaac and Rebecca, a.k.a. *The Jewish Bride*, c. 1665-1669

The man gently draws the woman toward him. She's comfortable enough with him to sink into thought, and she reaches up unconsciously to return the gentle touch. They're young but wizened. This uncommissioned portrait (its subjects remain unknown) is a truly human look at the relationship between two people in love. They form a protective pyramid of love amid a gloomy background. The touching hands form the center of this somewhat sad but peaceful work. Van Gogh said that "Rembrandt alone has that tenderness—the heartbroken tenderness."

Rembrandt was a master of oil painting. In his later years, he rendered details with a messier, more Impressionistic style. The red-brown-gold of the couple's clothes is a patchwork of oil laid on thick with a palette knife.

The Wardens of the Amsterdam Drapers Guild, a.k.a. *The Syndics*, 1662

Rembrandt could paint an official group portrait better than anyone.

Rembrandt's tender *Jewish Bride*

Drapers Guild—meeting interrupted

In the painting made famous by Dutch Masters cigars, he catches the Drapers Guild in a natural but dignified pose (dignified, at least, until the guy on the left sits on his friend's lap).

It's a business meeting, and they're all dressed in black with black hats—the standard power suit of the Dutch Golden Age. They gather around a table examining the company's books. Suddenly, someone (us) walks in, and they look up. It's as natural as a snapshot, though X-rays show Rembrandt made many changes in posing them perfectly.

The figures are "framed" by the table beneath them and the top of the wood paneling above their heads, making a three-part composition that brings this band of colleagues together. Even in this simple portrait, we feel we can read the guild members' personalities in their faces. (If the table in the painting looks like it's sloping a bit unnaturally, lie on the floor to view it at Rembrandt's intended angle.)

▸ *At the far end of the Gallery of Honor is the museum's star masterpiece. The best viewing spot is to the right of center—the angle Rembrandt had in mind when he designed it.*

The Night Watch, a.k.a. The Militia Company of Captain Frans Banninck Cocq, 1642

This is Rembrandt's most famous—though not necessarily greatest—painting. Created in 1642, when he was 36, it was one of his most important commissions: a group portrait of a company of Amsterdam's Civic Guards to hang in their meeting hall.

It's an action shot. With flags waving and drums beating, the guardsmen (who, by the 1640s, were really only an honorary militia of rich bigwigs) spill onto the street from under an arch in the back. It's "all for one and one for all" as they rush to Amsterdam's rescue. The soldiers grab lances and load their muskets. In the center, the commander (in black, with a red sash) strides forward energetically with a hand gesture that seems to say, "What are we waiting for? Let's move out!" His lieutenant focuses on his every order.

Rembrandt caught the optimistic spirit of Holland in the 1600s. Its war of independence from Spain was heading to victory and the economy was booming. These guardsmen on the move epitomize the proud, independent, upwardly mobile Dutch.

Why is *The Night Watch* so famous? Compare it with other, less famous group portraits nearby, where every face is visible and everyone

Rembrandt's famous *Night Watch*—Civic Guards in action

is well-lit, flat, and flashbulb-perfect. These people paid good money to have their mugs preserved for posterity, and they wanted it right up front. Other group portraits may be colorful, dignified works by a master...but not quite masterpieces.

By contrast, Rembrandt rousted the Civic Guards off their fat duffs. By adding movement and depth to an otherwise static scene, he took posers and turned them into warriors. He turned a simple portrait into great art.

OK, some *Night Watch* scuttlebutt: First off, "night watch" is a misnomer. It's a daytime scene, but over the years, as the preserving varnish darkened and layers of dirt built up, the sun set on this painting, and it got its popular title. When the painting was moved to a smaller room, the sides were lopped off (and the pieces lost), putting the two main characters in the center and causing the work to become more static than intended. During World War II, the painting was rolled up and hidden for five years. In 1975, a madman attacked the painting, slicing the captain's legs, and in 1990, it was sprayed with acid (it was skillfully restored after both incidents).

The Night Watch, contrary to popular myth, was a smashing success in its day. However, there are elements in it that show why Rembrandt soon fell out of favor as a portrait painter. He seemed to spend as much time painting the dwarf and the mysterious glowing girl with a chicken (the very appropriate mascot of this "militia" of shopkeepers) as he did the faces of his employers.

Rembrandt's life darkened long before his *Night Watch* did. This work marks the peak of Rembrandt's popularity...and the beginning of his fall from grace. He continued to paint masterpieces. Free from the dictates of employers whose taste was in their mouths, he painted what he wanted, how he wanted it. Rembrandt goes beyond mere craftsmanship to probe into, and draw life from, the deepest wells of the human soul.

▶ *Backtrack a few steps to the Gallery of Honor's last alcove to find Rembrandt's...*

Self-Portrait as the Apostle Paul, 1661

Rembrandt's many self-portraits show us the evolution of a great painter's style, as well as the progress of a genius's life. For Rembrandt, the two were intertwined.

In this somber, late self-portrait, the man is 55 but he looks 70. With a lined forehead, a bulbous nose, and messy hair, he peers out from under several coats of glazing, holding old, wrinkled pages. His look is...skeptical? Weary? Resigned to life's misfortunes? Or amused? (He's looking at us, but not *just* at us—remember that a self-portrait is done staring into a mirror.)

This man has seen it all—success, love, money, fatherhood, loss, poverty, death. He took these experiences and wove them into his art. Rembrandt died poor and misunderstood, but he remained very much his own man to the end.

▶ *You'll find more Rembrandts in Room 2.8, located a half-dozen rooms to the left of The Night Watch.*

Self-Portrait, c. 1628

Here we see the young small-town boy about to launch himself into whatever life has to offer. Rembrandt was a precocious kid. His father, a miller, insisted that he become a lawyer. His mother hoped he'd be a preacher (you may see a portrait of her reading the Bible). Rembrandt combined the secular and religious worlds by becoming an artist, someone who can hint at the spiritual by showing us the beauty of the created world.

He moved to Amsterdam and entered the highly competitive art world. Amsterdam was a booming town and, like today, a hip and

Self-Portrait: These eyes have seen it all.

Young Rembrandt—what does his future hold?

cosmopolitan city. Rembrandt portrays himself at age 22 as being divided—half in light, half hidden by hair and shadows—open-eyed, but wary of an uncertain future. Rembrandt's paintings are often light and dark, both in color and in subject, exploring the "darker" side of human experience.

Portrait of a Woman, Possibly Maria Trip, 1639

This debutante daughter of a wealthy citizen is shy and reserved—maybe a bit awkward in her new dress and adult role, but still self-assured. When he chose to, Rembrandt could dash off a commissioned portrait like nobody's business. The details are immaculate—the lace and shiny satin, the pearls behind the veil, the subtle face and hands. Rembrandt gives us not just a person, but a personality.

Look at the red rings around her eyes, a detail a lesser painter would have airbrushed out. Rembrandt takes this feature, unique to her, and uses it as a setting for her luminous, jewel-like eyes. Without being prettified, she's beautiful.

Young Woman in Fantasy Costume, Possibly Saskia, 1633

It didn't take long for Amsterdam to recognize Rembrandt's great talent. Everyone wanted a portrait done by the young master, and he became wealthy and famous. He fell in love with and married the rich, beautiful, and cultured Saskia. By all accounts, the two were enormously happy, entertaining friends, decorating their house with fine furniture, raising a family, and living the high life. In this painting, Saskia's face literally glows, and a dash of white paint puts a sparkle in her eye. Barely 30 years old, Rembrandt was the most successful painter in Holland. He had it all.

Jeremiah Lamenting the Destruction of Jerusalem, 1630

The Babylonians have sacked and burned Jerusalem, but Rembrandt leaves the pyrotechnics (in the murky background at left) to Spielberg and the big screen. Instead, he tells the story of Israel's destruction in the face of the prophet who predicted the disaster. Jeremiah slumps in defeat, deep in thought, confused and despondent, trying to understand why this evil had to happen. Rembrandt turns his floodlight of truth on the prophet's deeply lined forehead.

Rembrandt wasn't satisfied to crank out portraits of fat merchants in frilly bibs, no matter what they paid him. He wanted to experiment, trying new techniques and more probing subjects. Many of his paintings weren't commissioned and were never even intended for sale. His subjects could be brooding and melancholy, a bit dark for the public's taste. His technique set him apart—you can recognize a Rembrandt canvas by his play of light and dark. Most of his paintings are a deep brown tone, with only a few bright spots glowing from the darkness. This allowed Rembrandt to highlight the details he thought most important and to express moody emotions.

▶ *Finish your tour with another painting here in Room 2.8. It's a large group portrait by Bartholomeus van der Helst, called...*

The Banquet at the Crossbowmen's Guild, 1648

This colorful portrait of several dozen Amsterdammers was painted to celebrate Holland's new era of peace after its war with Spain. Though shown in military uniforms, these men were really captains of industry—shipbuilders, seamen, salesmen, spice tasters, bankers, and venture capitalists. This group portrait captures the prosperity and can-do spirit of the Dutch Golden Age.

Maria Trip radiates honest beauty.

Jeremiah—brooding in the darkness

Bartholomeus Van der Helst's glorious group portrait is just one of many Golden Age treasures.

The Rest of the Rijks

The museum is most famous for the paintings you've just seen. But with a collection of 8,000 works—detailing Dutch history from 1200 to the present—the Rijks offers much, much more.

Level 2: The second floor is home to more **Golden Age artifacts.** Keep circling the floor counterclockwise, keeping an eye out for a stunning collection of blue-and-white Delftware, dollhouses, and a big wooden model of a 74-gun Dutch man-of-war.

Level 1: There's a **Van Gogh self-portrait** that portrays him with the bright thick brushstrokes that would become his signature.

Level 0: This has everything from **women's fashion** to more Delftware. The **Asian Art** Pavilion shows off objects from the East Indies—a former Dutch colony—as well as items from India, Japan, Korea, and China.

Level 3: Finally, you could ride the elevator up to the top floor for exhibits from the **20th century,** including an airplane, bringing you up to the present.

Van Gogh Museum Tour

The Van Gogh Museum (we say "van GO," the Dutch say "van hock") is a cultural high even for those not into art. Located near the Rijksmuseum, the museum houses the 200 paintings owned by Vincent's younger brother, Theo. It's a user-friendly stroll through the work and life of one enigmatic man. If you like brightly colored landscapes in the Impressionist style, you'll like this museum. If you enjoy finding deeper meaning in works of art, you'll really love it. The mix of Van Gogh's creative genius, his tumultuous life, and the traveler's determination to connect to it makes this museum as much a walk with Vincent as with his art.

Cost: €18, covered by Museumkaart and I Amsterdam City Card. Tickets likely available online only (no in-person ticket sales), and even pass holders must reserve a time slot. Buy timed-entry tickets at www.vangoghmuseum.com (tickets go on sale about four months in advance).

Hours: Daily April-Aug 9:00-19:00, Fri until 21:00, Sat until 18:00 (April-June) and 21:00 (July-Aug); Sept-Oct 9:00-18:00, Fri until 21:00; Nov-March 9:00-17:00, Fri until 21:00. Confirm evening hours before you visit.

Information: Tel. 020/570-5200, www.vangoghmuseum.com.

Getting There: It's the big, modern, gray-and-beige place a few blocks behind the Rijksmuseum; visitors enter via a glass pavilion on the Museumplein. From Centraal Station, catch tram #2 or #12 to the Rijksmuseum or Van Baerlestraat stop.

Tours: The €5 multimedia guide gives insightful commentaries about Van Gogh's paintings and his technique, along with related quotations from Vincent himself.

Length of This Tour: Allow one hour.

Baggage Check: Free and mandatory.

Cuisine Art: The museum has a cafeteria-style café.

THE TOUR BEGINS

The collection is laid out roughly chronologically, through the changes in Vincent van Gogh's life and styles. You start on level 0, where

The Van Gogh Museum on Museumplein

Avoid crowds by visiting on Friday evening.

self-portraits introduce you to the artist. Level 1 has his early paintings; level 2 focuses on the man and his contemporaries; and level 3 has his final works.

▶ *Pass through security and the ticket booth into the glass-pavilion reception hall. Here you'll find an info desk, bag check, multimedia-guide rental, and WCs. Make your way up an escalator to the permanent collection, arriving on **level 0.***

Vincent van Gogh, 1853-1890

I am a man of passions...

You could see Vincent van Gogh's canvases as a series of suicide notes—or as the record of a life full of beauty...perhaps too full of beauty. He attacked life with a passion, experiencing highs and lows more intensely

Self-portraits capture Vincent at various stages of his short life.

than the average person. The beauty of the world overwhelmed him; its ugliness struck him as only another dimension of beauty. He tried to absorb the full spectrum of experience, good and bad, and channel it onto a canvas. The frustration of this overwhelming task drove him to madness. If all this is a bit overstated—and I guess it is—it's an attempt to show the emotional impact that Van Gogh's works have had on many people, me included.

Vincent, a pastor's son from a small Dutch town, started working at age 16 as a clerk for an art dealer. But his two interests, art and religion, distracted him from his dreary work, and after several years, he was fired.

The next 10 years were a collage of dead ends as he traveled northern Europe pursuing one path after another. He launched into each project with incredible energy, then became disillusioned and moved on to something else: teacher at a boarding school, assistant preacher, bookstore apprentice, preacher again, theology student, English student, literature student, art student. He bounced around England, France, Belgium, and the Netherlands. He fell in love but was rejected for someone more respectable. He quarreled with his family and was estranged. He lived with a prostitute and her daughter, offending the few friends he had. Finally, in his late twenties, worn out, flat broke, and in poor health, he returned to his family in Nuenen and made peace. He then started to paint.

▸ *Ascend to* **level 1**. *Work clockwise around the floor and follow the stages of Vincent's life. Start with his stark, dark early work.*

The Netherlands, 1880-1885

Peasants, Poverty, and Religion

These dark, gray-brown canvases show us the hard, plain existence of the people and town of Nuenen in the rural southern Netherlands. Van Gogh painted the town's simple buildings, bare or autumnal trees, and overcast skies—a world where it seems spring will never arrive. What warmth there is comes from the sturdy, gentle people themselves.

The style is crude—Van Gogh couldn't draw very well and would never become a great technician. The paint is laid on thick, as though painted with Nuenen mud. The main subject is almost always dead center, with little or no background, so there's a claustrophobic feeling. We are unable to see anything but the immediate surroundings.

The Potato Eaters, 1885

Those that prefer to see the peasants in their Sunday-best may do as they like. I personally am convinced I get better results by painting them in their roughness... If a peasant picture smells of bacon, smoke, potato steam—all right, that's healthy.

In a dark, cramped room lit only by a dim lamp, poor workers help themselves to a steaming plate of potatoes. They've earned it. Vincent deliberately wanted the canvas to be potato-colored.

He had dabbled as an artist during his wandering years, sketching things around him and taking a few art classes, but it wasn't until age 29 that Vincent painted his first oil canvas. He soon threw himself into it with abandon.

He painted the poor working peasants. He knew them well, having worked as a lay minister among peasants and miners. He joined them at work in the mines, taught their children, and even gave away his own few possessions to help them. The church authorities finally dismissed him for "excessive zeal," but he came away understanding the poor's harsh existence and the dignity with which they bore it.

Still Life with Bible, 1885

I have a terrible need of—shall I say the word?—religion. Then I go out and paint the stars.

The Bible and Émile Zola's *La Joie de Vivre*—these two books dominated Van Gogh's life. In his art he tried to fuse his religious upbringing with his love of the world's beauty. He lusted after life with a religious fervor. The burned-out candle tells us of the recent death of his father. The Bible is open to Isaiah 53: "He was despised and rejected of men, a man of sorrows..."

Potato Eaters—the peasants he worked with

Still Life with Bible—son of a minister

The Old Church Tower at Nuenen,
a.k.a. *The Peasants' Churchyard,* 1885

The crows circle above the local cemetery of Nuenen. Soon after his father's death, Vincent—in poor health and depressed—moved briefly to Antwerp. He then decided to visit his younger brother Theo, an art dealer living in Paris, the art capital of the world. Theo's support—financial and emotional—allowed Vincent to spend the rest of his short life painting.

Vincent moved from rural, religious, poor Holland to Paris, the City of Light. Vincent van Gone.

▶ *Continue to the room with work he did in...*

Paris, March 1886-February 1888

Impressionism

The sun begins to break through, lighting up everything he paints. His canvases are more colorful and the landscapes more spacious, with plenty of open sky, giving a feeling of exhilaration after the closed, dark world of Nuenen.

In the cafés and bars of Paris' bohemian Montmartre district, Vincent met the revolutionary Impressionists. He roomed with Theo and became friends with other struggling young painters, such as Paul Gauguin and Henri de Toulouse-Lautrec. His health improved. He became more sociable, had an affair with an older woman, and was generally happy.

He signed up to study under a well-known classical teacher but quit after only a few classes. He couldn't afford to hire models, so he roamed the streets, sketch pad in hand, and learned from his Impressionist friends.

The Impressionists emphasized getting out of the stuffy studio and setting up canvases outside on the street or in the countryside to paint the play of sunlight off the trees, buildings, and water.

As you see in this room, at first, Vincent copied from the Impressionist masters. He painted garden scenes like Claude Monet, café snapshots like Edgar Degas, "block prints" like the Japanese masters, and self-portraits like...nobody else.

Self-Portrait as a Painter, 1887-1888

I am now living with my brother Vincent, who is studying the art of painting with indefatigable zeal.

—Theo van Gogh to a friend

Here, the budding young artist proudly displays his new palette full of bright new colors, trying his hand at the Impressionist technique of building a scene using dabs of different-colored paint. A whole new world of art—and life—opened up to him in Paris.

Self-Portrait with Straw Hat, 1887

You wouldn't recognize Vincent, he has changed so much... The doctor says that he is now perfectly fit again. He is making tremendous strides with his work... He is also far livelier than he used to be and is popular with people.

—Theo van Gogh to their mother

In Paris, Vincent learned the Impressionist painting technique. The shimmering effect comes from placing dabs of different colors side by side on the canvas. At a distance, the two colors blend in the eye of the viewer to become a single color. Here, Vincent uses separate strokes of blue, yellow, green, and red to create a brown beard—but a brown that throbs with excitement.

Red Cabbages and Onions, 1887

Vincent quickly developed his own style: thicker paint; broad, swirling brushstrokes; and brighter, clashing colors that make even inanimate objects seem to pulsate with life. The many different colors are supposed to blend together, but you'd have to back up to Belgium to make these colors resolve into focus.

Gloomy church tower in hometown Nuenen

In Paris, the artist found bright colors.

Self-Portrait with Gray Felt Hat, 1887

He has painted one or two portraits which have turned out well, but he insists on working for nothing. It is a pity that he shows no desire to earn some money because he could easily do so here. But you can't change people.

—Theo van Gogh to their mother

Despite his new sociability, Vincent never quite fit in with his Impressionist friends. As he developed into a good painter, he became anxious to strike out on his own. He thought the social life of the big city was distracting him from serious work. In this painting, his face screams out from a swirling background of molecular activity. He wanted peace and quiet, a place where he could throw himself into his work completely. He headed for the sunny south of France.

▶ *Travel to the far end of the room, where you reach...*

Arles, February 1888-May 1889

Sunlight, Beauty, and Madness

Winter was just turning to spring when Vincent arrived in Arles, near the French Riviera. After the dreary Paris winter, the colors of springtime overwhelmed him. The blossoming trees and colorful fields inspired him to paint canvas after canvas, drenched in sunlight.

The Yellow House, a.k.a. The Street, 1888

It is my intention...to go temporarily to the South, where there is even more color, even more sun.

Vincent rented this house with the green shutters. (He ate at the pink café next door.) Look at that blue sky! He painted in a frenzy, working feverishly to try and take it all in. For the next nine months, he produced an explosion of canvases, working very quickly when the mood

With straw hat and pipe, he painted outdoors.

Traditional still life with modern colors

Thick brushstrokes radiate outward, magnifying the artist's ultra-intense gaze.

possessed him. His unique style evolved beyond Impressionism—thicker paint, stronger outlines, brighter colors (often applied right from the paint tube), and swirling brushwork that makes inanimate objects pulse and vibrate with life.

The Bedroom, 1888

I am a man of passions, capable of and subject to doing more or less foolish things—which I happen to regret, more or less, afterwards.
Vincent was alone, a Dutchman in Provence. And that had its downside. Vincent swung from flurries of ecstatic activity to bouts of great

loneliness. Like anyone traveling alone, he experienced those high highs and low lows. This narrow, trapezoid-shaped, single-room apartment (less than 200 square feet) must have seemed like a prison cell at times. (Psychologists have pointed out that most everything in this painting comes in pairs—two chairs, two paintings, a double bed squeezed down to a single—indicating his desire for a mate. Hmm.)

He invited his friend Paul Gauguin to join him, envisioning a sort of artists' colony in Arles. He spent months preparing a room upstairs for Gauguin's arrival.

Sunflowers, 1889

The worse I get along with people, the more I learn to have faith in Nature and concentrate on her.

Vincent saw sunflowers as his signature subject, and he painted a half-dozen versions of them, each a study in intense yellow. If he signed the work (look on the vase), it means he was proud of it.

Even a simple work like these sunflowers bursts with life. Different people see different things in *Sunflowers*. Is it a happy painting, or is it a melancholy one? Take your own emotional temperature and see.

The Sower, 1888

A dark, silhouetted figure sows seeds in the burning sun. It's late in the day. The heat from the sun, the source of all life, radiates out in thick swirls of paint. The sower must be a hopeful man, because the field looks slanted and barren. Someday, he thinks, the seeds he's planting will grow into something great, like the tree that slashes diagonally across the scene—tough and craggy, but with small, optimistic blossoms.

His *Yellow House* in sunny Arles

His bedroom, fit for the monastic artist

When Van Gogh signed a painting (like *Sunflowers*), it meant he was proud of it.

In his younger years, Vincent had worked in Belgium sowing the Christian gospel in a harsh environment (see Mark 4:1-9). Now in Arles, ignited by the sun, he cast his artistic seeds to the wind, hoping.

Gauguin's Chair, 1888

Empty chairs—there are many of them, there will be even more, and sooner or later, there will be nothing but empty chairs.

Gauguin arrived. At first, he and Vincent got along great. But then things went sour. They clashed over art, life, and their prickly personalities. On Christmas Eve 1888, Vincent went ballistic. Enraged during an alcohol-fueled argument, he pulled out a razor and waved it in Gauguin's face. Gauguin took the hint and quickly left town. Vincent was horrified at himself. In a fit of remorse and madness, he mutilated his own ear and presented it to a prostitute.

The people of Arles realized they had a madman on their hands. A doctor diagnosed "acute mania with hallucinations," and the local vicar talked Vincent into admitting himself to a peaceful mental hospital. Vincent wrote to Theo: "Temporarily I wish to remain shut up, as much for my own peace of mind as for other people's."

▶ *Ascend to* **level 2,** *which is less about Van Gogh's paintings than about his relationships with family and friends, and his artistic process. To see his final paintings, continue up to* **level 3.**

St-Rémy, May 1889-May 1890

The Mental Hospital

In the mental hospital, Vincent kept painting whenever he was well enough. He often couldn't go out, so he copied from books, making his own distinctive versions of works by Rembrandt, Delacroix, Millet, and others.

At first, the peace and quiet of the asylum did Vincent good, and his health improved. Occasionally, he was allowed outside to paint the gardens and landscapes. Meanwhile, the paintings he had been sending to Theo began to attract attention in Paris for the first time. A woman in Brussels bought one of his canvases—the only painting he ever sold during his lifetime. In 1987, one of his *Sunflowers* sold for $40 million. Three years later a portrait of Vincent's doctor went for more than $80 million.

At St-Rémy, we see a change from bright, happy landscapes to

Gauguin's Chair: When his friend visited, Vincent drove him away in a fit of madness.

more introspective subjects. The colors are less bright and more surreal, the brushwork even more furious. The strong outlines of figures are twisted and tortured.

The Garden of Saint Paul's Hospital, a.k.a. Leaf Fall, 1889
A traveler going to a destination that does not exist...
The stark brown trees are blown by the wind. A solitary figure (Vincent?) winds along a narrow, snaky path as the wind blows leaves on him. The colors are surreal—blue, green, and red tree trunks with heavy black outlines. A road runs away from us, heading nowhere.

The Sheaf Binder, after Millet, 1889
I want to paint men and women with that something of the eternal which the halo used to symbolize...
Vincent's compassion for honest laborers remained constant. These sturdy folk, with their curving bodies, wrestle as one with their curving wheat. The world Vincent sees is charged from within by spiritual fires, twisting and turning matter into energy, and vice versa.

Wheat Field with a Reaper, 1889
I have been working hard and fast in the last few days. This is how I try to express how desperately fast things pass in modern life.
The harvest is here. The time is short. There's much work to be done. A lone reaper works uphill, scything through a swirling wheat field, cutting slender paths of calm. Vincent saw the reaper—a figure of impending death—as the flip side of the sower.

Pietà, after Delacroix, 1889
It's evening after a thunderstorm. Jesus has been crucified, and the

Vincent portrays workers with noble dignity.

The trees ripple with an inner force.

corpse lies at the mouth of a tomb. Mary, whipped by the cold wind, holds her empty arms out in despair and confusion. She is the tender mother who receives us all in death, as though saying, "My child, you've been away so long—rest in my arms." Christ has a Vincent-esque red beard.

Auvers-sur-Oise, May–July 1890

The bird looks through the bars at the overcast sky where a thunderstorm is gathering, and inwardly he rebels against his fate. 'I am caged, I am caged, and you tell me I have everything I need! Oh! I beg you, give me liberty, that I may be a bird like other birds.' A certain idle man resembles this idle bird…

Though Van Gogh wished to be free of the mental hospital, his fits of madness would not relent. During these spells, he lost all sense of his own actions. He couldn't paint, the one thing he felt driven to do. He wrote to Theo, "My surroundings here begin to weigh on me more than I can say—I need air. I feel overwhelmed by boredom and grief."

Almond Blossom, 1890

Vincent moved north to Auvers, a small town near Paris where he could stay under a doctor-friend's supervision. On the way there, he visited Theo. Theo's wife had just had a baby, whom they named Vincent. Brother Vincent showed up with this painting under his arm as a birthday gift. Theo's wife later recalled, "I had expected a sick man, but here was a sturdy, broad-shouldered man with a healthy color, a smile on his face, and a very resolute appearance."

In his new surroundings, he continued painting, averaging a canvas a day, but was interrupted by spells that swung from boredom to

This pietà creates a mystical mood.

The fleeting glory of the *Almond Blossom*

Vincent's last painting is of a field, like the one where he would end his short life.

madness. His letters to Theo were generally optimistic, but he worried that he'd soon succumb completely to insanity and never paint again.

▶ *Vincent's final landscapes are walls of bright, thick paint. Nature is charged from within with a swirling energy.*

Wheat Field with Crows, 1890

This new attack...came on me in the fields, on a windy day, when I was busy painting.

On July 27, 1890, Vincent left his room, walked out to a nearby field, and put a bullet through his chest.

This is one of the last paintings Vincent finished. We can try to search the wreckage of his life for the black box explaining what happened, but there's not much there. His life was sad and tragic, but the record he left is one not of sadness, but of beauty—intense beauty. The windblown wheat field is a nest of restless energy. Scenes like this must have overwhelmed Vincent with their incredible beauty—too much, too fast, with no release. The sky is stormy and dark blue, almost nighttime, barely lit by two suns boiling through the deep ocean of blue. The road starts nowhere, leads nowhere, disappearing into the burning wheat field. Above all of this swirling beauty fly the crows, the dark ghosts that had hovered over his life since the cemetery in Nuenen.

Red Light District Walk

Amsterdam's oldest neighborhood has hosted the world's oldest profession since the Middle Ages. Today, prostitution and public marijuana use thrive here, creating a spectacle that's unique in all of Europe.

On our walk, we'll see history, sleaze, and cheese: transvestites in windows, drunks in doorways, and cannabis in bongs. The main event is sex: prostitutes in bras, thongs, and high heels, standing in window displays, offering their bodies—and it's all legal.

Not for Everyone: The Red Light District seems to have something to offend everyone. Whether it's in-your-face images of graphic sex, exploited immigrant women, whips and chains, passed-out drug addicts, the pungent smells of pot and urine, or just the shameless commercialism of it all, it's not everyone's cup of tea. And though I encourage people to expand their horizons, it's perfectly OK to say, "No, thank you."

ORIENTATION

Length of This Walk: Allow two hours.

Photography: Don't take photos of women in windows—even with an inconspicuous phone camera—or a snarly bouncer may appear from out of nowhere to forcibly rip it from your hands. Photos of landmarks are OK, but remember that a camera is a prime target in this high-theft area.

When to Go: The best times to visit are afternoons and early evenings. Avoid late nights (after about 22:30), when the tourists disappear and the area gets creepy.

Safety: If you're on the ball and smart, you'll find that it's quite safe. The neighborhood is slowly gentrifying and police on horseback keep things orderly. But there are plenty of rowdy drunks, drug-pushing lowlifes, con artists, and pickpockets. Assume any fight or commotion is a ploy to distract innocent victims who are about to lose their wallets.

Old Church (Oude Kerk): Church—€10 (credit cards only), Mon-Sat 10:00-18:00, Sun 13:00-17:30. Tower climb—€7.50 with 30-minute tour, April-Oct Mon-Sat 12:00-18:00.

Prostitution Information Center (PIC): €1, Wed-Sat 12:00-17:00, closed Sun-Tue, €17.50 walking tours offered Wed, Fri, and Sat at 17:00, cash only, tel. 020/420-7328, www.pic-amsterdam.com.

Our Lord in the Attic Museum: €11, Mon-Sat 10:00-18:00, Sun from 13:00.

Cannabis College: Free, daily 11:00-19:00.

Hemp Gallery and Hash, Marijuana, and Hemp Museum: €9, daily 10:00-22:00.

Tours: 🎧 Download my free Red Light District audio tour. The PIC also offers tours (see above).

THE WALK BEGINS

▶ *Start on Dam Square. Face the big, fancy Grand Hotel Krasnapolsky. To the left of the hotel stretches the long street called...*

❶ Warmoesstraat

You're walking along one of the city's oldest streets, the traditional border of the Red Light District.

▶ *Our first stop is the small shop with the large, yellow triangle sign, about 100 yards down on the right at #141.*

❷ Condomerie

Located at the entrance to the Red Light District, this is the perfect place to get prepared. Besides selling an amazing variety of condoms, this shop has a knack for entertainment, working to make their front window display appropriate to the season. A three-ring notebook on the counter shows off all the inventory.

▶ *From here, pass the two little street barricades with cute red lights around them and enter the traffic-free world of...*

❸ De Wallen

Amsterdammers call this area De Wallen ("The Walls"), after the old retaining walls that once stood here. It's the oldest part of town, with the oldest church. It grew up between the harbor and Dam Square, where the city was born. Amsterdam was a port town, located where the river met the sea. The city traded in all kinds of goods, including things popular with sailors and businessmen away from home—like sex and drugs.

Condom shop—be prepared.

Smartshops sell natural hallucinogens.

According to legend, Quentin Tarantino holed up at the Winston Hotel (at #129) for three months in 1993 to write *Pulp Fiction*. The neighborhood attracts many out-of-towners, especially Brits, who catch cheap flights here for "stag" (bachelor) parties or just a wild weekend—and the Dutch accommodate them with Irish pubs and football matches on TVs in the bars.

▶ *Continue down Warmoesstraat a few more steps. At #97 is the...*

❹ Elements of Nature Smartshop

This "smartshop" is a clean, well-lit, fully professional retail outlet that sells powerful drugs, many of which are illegal in America. Products are clearly marked with prices, brief descriptions, ingredients, and effects. The knowledgeable salespeople can give you more information on their "100 percent natural products that play with the human senses."

Their "natural" drugs include harmless nutrition boosters (such as royal jelly), harmful but familiar tobacco, and herbal versions of popular dance-club drugs (such as herbal Ecstasy). Marijuana seeds are the big sellers.

▶ *Continue a bit farther down Warmoesstraat, to an area filled with...*

❺ Sex Shops

Throughout the district, various sex-shop retail outlets deal in erotic paraphernalia (dildos, S&M starter kits, kinky magazines) and offer video booths with porn films. While Amsterdam is notorious for its Red Light District, even small Dutch towns often have a sex shop and a brothel to satisfy their citizens' needs.

▶ *Backtrack a few steps to the intersection, and head down Wijde Kerksteeg to the...*

❻ Old Church (Oude Kerk)

As the name implies, this was the medieval city's original church. Returning from a long sea voyage, sailors of yore would spy the steeple of the Old Church on the horizon and know they were home. Having returned safely, they'd come here to give thanks to St. Nicholas—the patron saint of this church, of seafarers, of Christmas, and of the city of Amsterdam.

Church construction began in the early 1200s—starting with a humble wooden chapel that expanded into a stone structure by the time it was consecrated in 1306. It was added onto in fits and starts for the next 200 years—as is apparent in the building's many gangly parts. Then, in the 15th century, Amsterdam built the New Church (Nieuwe Kerk) on Dam Square. But the Old Church still had the tallest spire, the biggest organ, and the most side-altars, and remained the city's center of activity, bustling inside and out with merchants and street markets.

The **tower** is 290 feet high, with an octagonal steeple atop a bell tower (you can pay to climb to the top). This tower served as the model for many other Dutch steeples. The carillon has 47 bells, which can chime mechanically or be played by one of Amsterdam's three official carillonneurs.

Circle to the right to the church entrance. While the church is historic, there's not much to see inside other than 2,500 gravestones in the floor (the most famous is for Rembrandt's wife, Saskia).

Nowadays, the church is the holy needle around which the unholy Red Light District spins. This marks the neighborhood's most dense concentration of prostitution.

Back outside, explore around the right side of the church. You'll see a **statue,** dedicated to the Unknown Prostitute. Attached to the church like barnacles are **small buildings.** These were originally used as homes for priests, church offices, or rental units. The house to the right of the entrance (at #25) is very tiny—32 feet by 8 feet.

The green metal structure over by the canal is a public **urinal.** It offers just enough privacy.

▶ *From the urinal, go a half-block south along the canal toward the...*

Old Church—historic charm amid the sleaze

Statue honoring the Unknown Prostitute

Red Light District Walk

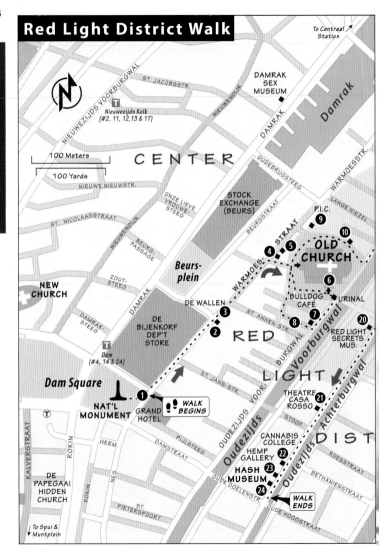

To Centraal Station

N

ST. JACOBSSTR.

NIEUWEZIJDS VOORBURGWAL

Nieuwezijds Kolk
(#2, 11, 12, 13 & 17)

NIEUWENDIJK

DAMRAK SEX MUSEUM

Damrak

DAMRAK

100 Meters

100 Yards

NIEUWE NIEUWSTR.

CENTER

OUDEBRUGSTEEG

WARMOESSTR.

ONZE LIEVE VROUWE STEEG

ST. NICOLAASSTRAAT

NIEUWENDIJK

BEURS-PASSAGE

STOCK EXCHANGE (BEURS)

BEURSSTRAAT

WARMOES- STRAAT

LANGE NIEZEL

P.I.C.
9

10

OLD CHURCH

NEW CHURCH

ZOUT-STEEG

DAMRAK

Beurs-plein

4 5

6

DAMRAK-STEEG

Dam
(#4, 14 & 24)

DE BIJENKORF DEP'T STORE

DE WALLEN

3

2

ST. ANNEN-STR.

BURGWAL

RED

BULLDOG CAFÉ

8 7

URINAL

20

RED LIGHT SECRETS MUS.

Voorburgwal

Achterburgwal

Dam Square

NAT'L MONUMENT

GRAND HOTEL

ST. JANS-STR.

1

WALK BEGINS

LIGHT

DIST

HERM.

KALVERSTRAAT

ROKIN

PIJLSTEEG

DAMSTRAAT

OUDEZIJDS VOOR. BURGWAL

THEATRE CASA ROSSO
21

STOOF

DE PAPEGAAI HIDDEN CHURCH

NES

ST. PIETERSPOORT

CANNABIS COLLEGE

HEMP GALLERY
22

HASH MUSEUM
23

24

OUDE DOELENSTR.

KOESSTRAAT

BETHANIENSTRAAT

OUDE HOOGSTRAAT

WALK ENDS

To Spui & Muntplein

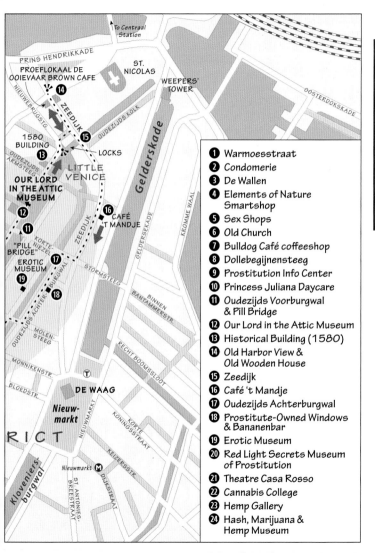

1 Warmoesstraat
2 Condomerie
3 De Wallen
4 Elements of Nature Smartshop
5 Sex Shops
6 Old Church
7 Bulldog Café coffeeshop
8 Dollebegijnensteeg
9 Prostitution Info Center
10 Princess Juliana Daycare
11 Oudezijds Voorburgwal & Pill Bridge
12 Our Lord in the Attic Museum
13 Historical Building (1580)
14 Old Harbor View & Old Wooden House
15 Zeedijk
16 Café 't Mandje
17 Oudezijds Achterburgwal
18 Prostitute-Owned Windows & Bananenbar
19 Erotic Museum
20 Red Light Secrets Museum of Prostitution
21 Theatre Casa Rosso
22 Cannabis College
23 Hemp Gallery
24 Hash, Marijuana & Hemp Museum

❼ Bulldog Café coffeeshop

The Bulldog claims to be Amsterdam's very first marijuana coffee-shop, established here in 1975. Now there's a chain of Bulldogs around the city. At "coffeeshops" like this one, customers start the transaction by asking the bartender, "Can I see the cannabis menu?" Then the bartender pulls out a display case with different varieties of weed, sold in baggies or prerolled joints. It's all clearly priced, and available either to-go or to smoke on the premises. You'll see people at the Bulldog enjoying a joint while they sip a beer or a Coke. As coffeeshops go, the Bulldog is considered pretty touristy—connoisseurs seek out smaller places with better-quality pot.

The political winds regarding cannabis are always shifting. Some Dutch leaders propose forbidding sales to nonresidents, hoping to discourage European drug dealers from buying pot to sell illegally in their home countries. But such a law would be devastating for businesses that depend on out-of-towners, so many Amsterdam politicians favor keeping pot legal.

▶ *Time to dive into the heart of the Red Light District. On the other side of the Bulldog, to the left, find the narrow alleyway called...*

❽ Dollebegijnensteeg

You're right in the thick of high-density prostitution. Remember: Don't take any pictures, and watch for pickpockets if crowds jostle together. If you do both these things, you'll be fine.

As you pass window after window of women in panties and bras, notice how they wink at the horny men, rap on the window to attract attention, text their friends, or look disdainfully at sightseers. You can

Marijuana coffeeshop—no big deal here

Narrow alley with prostitutes in windows

take your time here and then explore deeper (or you can hurry to the end of the block and turn right to return to the Old Church).

▶ *Return to the Old Church and start to circle the church clockwise. Around the back, you'll see older, plumper (and cheaper) prostitutes. In the same area, at Enge Kerksteeg 3, is the...*

❾ Prostitution Information Center (PIC)

This information center exists solely to demystify prostitution, giving visitors matter-of-fact information on how the trade works and what it's like to be a sex worker. It doles out pamphlets, books, condoms, T-shirts, and other offbeat souvenirs, and offers walking tours. They have a map showing exactly where prostitution is legal, and sell a small, frank booklet answering the most common questions tourists have about Amsterdam's Red Light District.

Nearby is a room-rental office (labeled *Kamerverhuurbedrijf*). Prostitutes come here to rent window space and bedrooms to use for their work. The office also sells work supplies—condoms by the case, toilet tissue, and lubricants. This office does not arrange sex. The women who rent space from this business are self-employed and negotiate directly with their customers.

In return for their rental fees, prostitutes get security. The rental office provides constant video surveillance. (You may see small cameras and orange alarm lights above many windows.) If prostitutes have any trouble, they press a buzzer that swiftly calls a burly bouncer or the police. The area sure looks rough, but aside from tricky pickpockets these streets are actually pretty safe.

▶ *Continue circling clockwise around the church. Amid prostitutes in*

Red Light areas have strict security video.

The "PIC" has info about the sex trade.

windows, find the white brick building on the left at Oudekerksplein 8. This is the...

❿ Princess Juliana Daycare

De Wallen is also a residential neighborhood, where ordinary citizens go about their daily lives. Of course, locals need someplace to send their kids. The Princess Juliana Daycare is for newborns to four-year-olds. It was built in the 1970s, when the idea was to mix all dimensions of society together, absorbing the seedy into the decent. I don't know about you, but this location would be a tough sell where I come from.

▶ *Turn left at the canal and continue north along...*

⓫ Oudezijds Voorburgwal and Pill Bridge

Pause at Pill Bridge and enjoy the canal and all the old buildings with their charming gables. Back in the 1970s, this bridge was nicknamed for the retail items sold by the seedy guys who used to hang out here. Now it's a pleasant place for a photo op.

▶ *Just past the bridge, at Oudezijds Voorburgwal 38, is one of the city's most worthwhile museums.*

⓬ Our Lord in the Attic Museum

With its triangular gable, this building looks like just another town-house. But inside, it holds a secret—a small, lavishly decorated place of worship hidden in the attic. Although Amsterdam has long been known for its tolerance, back in the 16th and 17th centuries there was one group they kept in the closet—Catholics. (For more, see page 130.)

▶ *Near the next bridge, on your left at #14, is an old brick building with red shutters.*

⓭ Historical Building

As we stroll up the canal, remember that this neighborhood is Amsterdam's oldest. It sits on formerly marshy land that was reclaimed by diking off the sea's tidal surge. That location gave Amsterdam's merchants easy access to both river trade and the North Sea. This building dates from that very era—around 1580.

The part of the canal we're walking along now is known as **"Little Venice"** (a term used Europe-wide for any charming neighborhood with canalside houses). Houses rise directly from the water here, with no quays or streets.

Prostitution 101

The prostitutes here are self-employed—entrepreneurs, renting space and running their own business. They usually work a four- to eight-hour shift. A good spot costs about €100 for a day shift, and €150 for an evening. Prostitutes are required to keep their premises hygienic, make sure their clients use condoms, and avoid minors.

Popular prostitutes can make about €500 a day. They fill out tax returns, and many belong to a loose union called the Red Thread. The law, not pimps, protects prostitutes. If a prostitute is diagnosed with HIV or AIDS, she loses her license. As shocking as legalized prostitution may seem to some, it's a good example of a pragmatic Dutch solution to a persistent problem.

Although some women choose prostitution as a lucrative career, others (some say most) are forced into it by circumstance—poverty, drug addiction, abusive men, and immigration scams. While the hope here in the Netherlands is that sex workers are smartly regulated small-businesspeople, in reality the line between victim and entrepreneur is not always so clear.

With a vision of "gentrification by design," Amsterdam's city government is splicing "legitimate" businesses into a district that for centuries has relied on only one product. As many as half of the sex businesses here may close over the next few years. A major Red Light District landlord was essentially given the option either to lease many of his booths to the city or be zoned out of business. The city picked up the leases, and windows that once showcased "girls for rent" now showcase mannequins wearing the latest fashions—lit by lights that aren't red.

▶ *At the end of the canal, continue straight up a small inclined lane called Sint Olofssteeg. At the top, turn left and walk along the street called Zeedijk. Go about 100 yards to the end of the block, where it opens up to an...*

⑭ Old Harbor View and Old Wooden House

As you survey the urban scene of today's Damrak and Centraal Station, imagine the scene as it looked in the 1600s. What today is mostly concrete was once the city's harbor. Boats sailed in and out of the harbor through an opening located where the train station sits now (on reclaimed land). From there, ships could sail along the IJ River out to the North Sea.

The **old wooden house** near here (at Zeedijk 1, now a café) was once a tavern, sitting right at what was then the water's edge.

Picture a ship tying up in the harbor. The crew has just returned home from a two-year voyage to Bali. They're bringing home fabulous wealth—crates and crates of spices, coffee, and silk. Sailors are celebrating their homecoming, spilling onto Zeedijk. Here they're greeted by swinging ladies swinging red lanterns. Their first stop might be nearby St. Olaf's chapel to say a prayer of thanks—or perhaps they head straight to this tavern at Zeedijk 1 and drop anchor for a good Dutch beer. Ahh-hh!

▶ *But our journey continues on. Backtrack along the same street, to the crest of a bridge, on…*

⑮ Zeedijk

The waterway below you is part of the city's system of locks: Once a day a worker opens up the box at the far end of the bridge, on the right, and presses a button. The locks open, and the tides flush out the city's canals. Look down—if the gate is open, you might see water flowing in or out. Zeedijk street runs along the top of the sea dike. It also connected the harbor, bustling with ocean-going ships, with De Wallen.

In the early 1600s, Zeedijk was thriving with overseas trade. But

Pill Bridge, near quaint Little Venice

Pioneering gay bar along Zeedijk street

Amsterdam would soon lose its maritime supremacy to England and France, and De Wallen never really recovered. By the 1970s, Zeedijk had become unbelievably sleazy. The area was a no-man's-land of junkies fighting among themselves, and the police just kept their distance.

But locals longed to take back this historic corner of their city and got to work. First, they legalized marijuana and then cracked down on hard drugs—heroin, cocaine, and pills. Almost overnight, the illicit drug trade dropped dramatically. Dealers got stiff sentences. Addicts got treatment. Four decades later, the policy seems to have worked. Zeedijk belongs to the people of Amsterdam once again.

▶ *Pause at #63, on the left.*

⓰ Café 't Mandje

This is one of Europe's first gay bars. It opened in 1927, closed in 1985, and is now a working bar once again. It stands as a memorial to the woman who ran it during its heyday in the 1950s and '60s: Bet van Beeren. Bet was a lesbian, and her bar became a hangout for gay people. Neckties hang from the ceiling, a reminder of Bet's tradition of scissoring off customers' ties.

▶ *Round the bend on Zeedijk street. Then make the next right and head a few steps down narrow Korte Stormsteeg street, back to the canalside red lights. Go left, walking along the left side of the canal.*

⓱ Oudezijds Achterburgwal

We're back in the glitzy Red Light District. This beautiful, tree-lined canal is the heart of this neighborhood's nightlife, playing host to most of the main nightclubs.

▶ *Make your way down the street's left-hand side. After about 30 yards, pause at the alleyway called Boomsteeg.*

⓲ Prostitute-Owned Windows and Bananenbar

Many of the prostitution windows near here (see Oudesijds #17, #19, and #27) are run by a cooperative of entrepreneurial prostitutes to create nice rooms for their clients and good working conditions for themselves—such as a lounge for sex workers between shifts.

Continue a few yards to #37 ("Banana Bar"). This popular nightclub's erotic Art Nouveau facade is far classier than what's offered

Social Control

De Wallen has pioneered the Dutch concept of "social control." In Holland, neighborhood security doesn't come from just the police, but from neighbors looking out for each another. If Geert doesn't buy bread for two days, the baker asks around if anyone's seen him. An elderly man feels safe in his home, knowing he's being watched over by the prostitutes next door. Unlike many big cities, there's no chance that anyone here could die or be in trouble and go unnoticed. Video-surveillance cameras keep an eye on the streets. So do prostitutes, who buzz for help if they spot trouble. As you stroll, watch the men who watch the women who watch out for their neighbors—"social control."

inside. For €60 you get admission for an hour, drinks included. Undressed ladies serve the drinks, perched on the bar. No touching, but you can order a banana and she'll serve it to you any way you like. For details, step into the lobby.

▶ *At Molensteeg, cross the bridge and look to the right.*

⑲ Erotic Museum

If it's graphic sex you seek, this is not the place. To put it bluntly, this museum is not very good (the Damrak Sex Museum on page 131 is better). However, it does offer a peek at some of the sex services found in the Red Light District. Displays include reconstructions of a prostitute's chambers, sex-shop windows, and videos of nightclub sex shows (on the third floor).

▶ *From the bridge, turn left and walk south along Oudezijds Achterburgwal. At #60H is the...*

⑳ Red Light Secrets Museum of Prostitution

Though overpriced, this museum is an earnest and mildly educational behind-the-scenes look at prostitution. You'll walk through a typical (tiny) room where prostitutes stand at the window, and a typical (tiny) back room with a bed and sink. Perhaps most thought-provoking: a video giving you the point of view of a sex worker as browsers check you out.

▶ *Continuing south, you'll pass two Casa Rosso franchises a block apart. The larger, lined by pink elephants, is...*

㉑ Theatre Casa Rosso

This is the Red Light District's best-known nightclub for live sex shows. Audience members pay a single price that includes drinks and a show. On stage, naked people engage in sex acts—some simulated, some completely real (€50, tickets cheaper online).

As you continue south along the canal, you gotta wonder: Why does Amsterdam embrace prostitution and drugs? It's not that the Dutch are more liberal in their attitudes, they're simply more pragmatic. They've found that when the sex trade goes underground, you get pimps, mobsters, and the spread of STDs. When marijuana is illegal, you get drug dealers, gangs, and violent turf wars. Their solution is to minimize problems through strict regulation.

▶ *But enough about sex. Let's talk about drugs. Along the right side of the next block, you'll find four cannabis-related establishments.*

Scenic canals and sex shows

㉒ Cannabis College

This free, nonprofit public study center aims to explain the pros and cons (but mostly pros) of the industrial, medicinal, and recreational uses of the green stuff. You can read about practical hemp products, the medical uses of marijuana, and police prosecution/persecution of cannabis users. For a €3 donation, you can visit the organic flowering cannabis garden downstairs.

▶ Continue up the street to #130, the...

㉓ Hemp Gallery

One ticket admits you to both the Hemp Gallery and the Hash, Marijuana, and Hemp Museum (described next). If you have the patience to read its thorough displays, you'll learn plenty about how valuable the cannabis plant was to Holland during the Golden Age. The leafy, green cannabis plant was grown on large plantations. The fibrous stalks (hemp) were made into rope and canvas for ships, and even used to make clothing and lace.

▶ Next is our last stop at #148, the...

In the evening, the area is safe and festive.

Several sights teach about marijuana...

...and its notorious history.

㉔ Hash, Marijuana, and Hemp Museum

This museum treats marijuana like it deserves scholarly study. The exhibits are quite extensive and interesting. The highlight is the grow room, where you look through windows at live cannabis plants in various stages of growth, some as tall as I am. At a certain stage they're "sexed" to weed out the boring males and "selected" to produce the most powerful strains. At the exit you'll pass through the **Sensi Seed Bank Store,** which sells weed seeds, how-to books, and knickknacks geared to growers.

Congratulations

We've seen a lot—from prostitutes to drug pushers to the ghosts of pioneer lesbians to politically active heads with green thumbs. We've talked a bit of history and politics, and a lot of sleaze. Now, go back to your hotel and take a shower.

Jordaan Walk

This walk takes you from Dam Square—the Times Square of Amsterdam—to the Anne Frank House, and then deep into the characteristic Jordaan neighborhood. Cafés, boutiques, bookstores, and art galleries have gentrified the area. On this cultural scavenger hunt, you'll experience the laid-back Dutch lifestyle and catch a few intimate details that most busy tourists never appreciate. You'll see things in the Jordaan (yor-DAHN) that are commonplace in no other city in the world.

Allow about 1.5 hours for this short and easygoing walk. It's best by day (before 18:00), when views are nice, and shops and sights are open. (St. Andrew's Courtyard is closed on Sundays.) Bring your camera, as you'll enjoy some of Amsterdam's most charming canal scenes.

🎧 Download my free Jordaan Walk audio tour.

THE WALK BEGINS

❶ Dam Square

Start in Dam Square, where the city was born (for more on this square, see page 20). The original residents settled east of here, in the De Wallen neighborhood (now the Red Light District). But as Amsterdam grew—from a river-trading village to a worldwide seagoing empire—the population needed new places to live. Citizens started reclaiming land to the west of Dam Square and built a "new church" (Nieuwe Kerk) to serve these new neighborhoods. Over time they needed still more land and continued to push westward. Canal by canal, they created waterways lined with merchants' townhouses.

By the 1600s—Amsterdam's Golden Age—residents had moved even farther west, building an even newer church called the Westerkerk (Western Church). The residential neighborhood around it is what we'll explore on this walk—the Jordaan.

▶ *Facing the Royal Palace, slip (to the right) between the palace and New Church. Check out the red-and-white brick building—the **Magna Plaza mall.** When it was built in 1899, it was Amsterdam's main post office and was constructed atop a foundation of pilings—some 4,500 of them. Facing Magna Plaza, head right, walking 50 yards down the busy street to the corner of a tiny street called...*

❷ Molsteeg

Scan the higgledy-piggledy facades along the busy street. Are you drunk, high...or just in Amsterdam, where the houses were built on mud? Check out the nice line of gables in this row of houses.

Before moving on, notice the T-shirt gallery on the corner. Decades ago, I bought a **Mark Raven** T-shirt from a street vendor. Now this Amsterdam original has his own upscale shop, selling T-shirts and paintings featuring spindly lined, semi-abstract cityscapes.

▶ *Now head left down tiny Molsteeg street—but don't walk on the reddish pavement in the middle; that's for bikes. From here this tour's essentially a straight shot west, though the street changes names along the way.*

A few steps along, on the left, find house #5: It's from 1644. Just one window wide, it's typical of the city's narrow old merchants' houses, with a shop on the ground floor, living space in the middle,

Start on Dam Square, face west, and walk.

Molsteeg is bike-friendly (so watch out!).

and storage in the attic. Look up to see the hooks above warehouse doors. Houses like this lean out toward the street on purpose, so you can hoist cargo (or a sofa) without banging it against the house.

At the intersection with Spuistraat, you'll likely see rows of **bicycles** parked along the street. Amsterdam's 850,000 residents own nearly that many bikes. Many people own two—a long-distance racing bike and an in-city bike, often deliberately kept in poor maintenance so it's less enticing to bike thieves. Locals are diligent about locking their bikes twice: They lock the spokes with the first lock, and then chain the bike to something immovable, such as a city hitching rack.

Amsterdam is a great bike town—and indeed, bikes outnumber cars. The efficient Dutch appreciate a self-propelled machine that travels five times faster than a person on foot, while creating zero pollution, noise, parking problems, or high fuel costs. On a *fiets* (bike), a speedy local can traverse the historic center in about 10 minutes. Biking seems to keep the populace fit and good-looking—people here say that Amsterdam's health clubs are more for networking than for working out.

▸ *After one more block, the street opens onto a small space that's actually a bridge, straddling the Singel canal. It's called...*

❸ Torensluis Bridge

We haven't quite reached the Jordaan yet, but the atmosphere already seems miles away from busy Dam Square. With cafés, art galleries, and fine benches for picnics, this is a great place to relax and take in a Golden Age atmosphere.

Singel Canal: This canal was the original moat running around

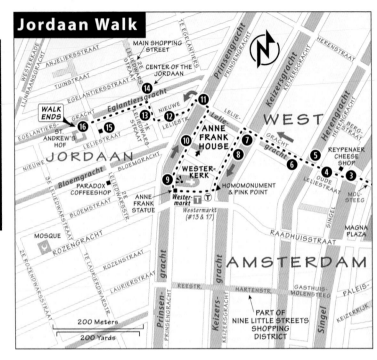

Jordaan Walk

the old walled city. This bridge is so wide because it was the road that led to one of the original city gates.

The Houses: The area still looks much as it might have during the Dutch Golden Age of the 1600s, when Amsterdam's seagoing merchants ruled the waves. Fueled with wealth, the city quickly became a major urban center, filled with impressive homes.

The houses crowd together, shoulder-to-shoulder. They're built on top of thousands of logs hammered vertically into the marshy soil to provide a foundation. Over the years, they've shifted with the tides, leaving some leaning this way and that. Notice that some of the brick houses have iron rods strapped onto the sides. These act like braces, binding the bricks to an inner skeleton of wood. Almost all Amsterdam houses have big, tall windows to let in as much light as possible.

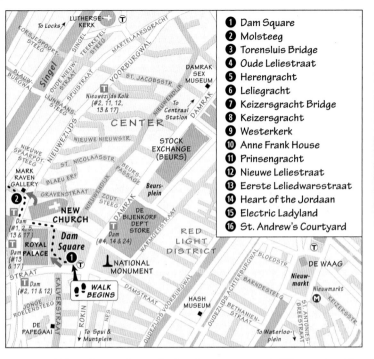

1 Dam Square
2 Molsteeg
3 Torensluis Bridge
4 Oude Leliestraat
5 Herengracht
6 Leliegracht
7 Keizersgracht Bridge
8 Keizersgracht
9 Westerkerk
10 Anne Frank House
11 Prinsengracht
12 Nieuwe Leliestraat
13 Eerste Leliedwarsstraat
14 Heart of the Jordaan
15 Electric Ladyland
16 St. Andrew's Courtyard

Although some houses look quite narrow, most of them extend far back. The rear of the building—called the *achterhuis*—is often much more spacious than you might expect. Real estate has always been expensive on this canal, where buildings were taxed on the width of their street frontage.

Multatuli: The "big head" statue honors a writer known by his pen name: Multatuli. Born in Amsterdam in 1820, Multatuli (a.k.a. Eduard Douwes Dekker) did what many young Dutchmen did back then: He sought his fortune in the East Indies, then a colony of the Netherlands. He witnessed firsthand the hard life of Javanese natives slaving away on Dutch-owned plantations. His semi-autobiographical novel, *Max Havelaar* (1860), follows a progressive civil servant

Playful Jordaan residents

Torensluis Bridge—cafés and views

fighting to reform colonial abuses. He was the first author to criticize Dutch colonial practices.

The Locks: In the distance, way down at the north end of the Singel, beyond the dome, you can glimpse one of the canal's **locks.** Those white-flagpole thingies, sprouting at 45-degree angles, are part of the apparatus that opens and shuts the gates. While the canals originated as a way to drain diked-off marshland, they eventually became part of the city's sewer system. They were flushed daily: Just open the locks and let the North Sea tides come in and out.

The Dutch are credited with inventing locks in the 1300s. (Let's not ask the Chinese.) Besides controlling water flow in the city, they allow ships to pass from higher to lower water levels, and vice versa. It's because of locks that you can ship something by boat from here inland. From this very spot, you could hop a boat and go upriver, connect to the Rhine, and eventually—over the continental divide in Germany—connect to the Danube and then sail to Romania and the Black Sea.

▶ *Continue west on...*

❹ Oude Leliestraat

On "Old Lily Street," consumers will find plenty of Amsterdam treats—Reypenaer's cheeses, Puccini's bonbons, Tuscany's sausages, Grey Area's marijuana, California's burritos, sushi, shoarmas—everything but lilies. The Reypenaer cheese shop is especially worthwhile, as it offers samples and tasting sessions (for a fee, reserve at www.reypenaer.com).

The Grey Area is a thriving coffeeshop; like Holland's other

Gables

Along the rooftops, Amsterdam's famous gables are false fronts to enhance roofs that are, generally, sharply pitched. Gables come in all shapes and sizes. They might be ornamented with animal and human heads, garlands, urns, scrolls, and curlicues. Despite their infinite variety, most belong to a few distinct types. See how many of these you can spot.

A simple "point" gable just follows the triangular shape of a normal pitched roof. A "bell" gable is shaped like...well, guess. "Step" gables are triangular in shape and lined with steps. The one with a rectangular protrusion at the peak is called a "spout" gable. "Neck" gables rise up vertically from a pair of sloping "shoulders." "Cornice" gables make pointed roofs look classically horizontal. (There's probably even a "clark" gable, but frankly, I don't give a damn.)

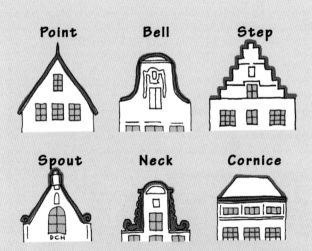

Point   Bell   Step

Spout   Neck   Cornice

"coffeeshops," it sells marijuana. The green-and-white decal in the window identifies it as #092 in the city's licensing program. While smoking marijuana is essentially legal here, the café's name refers to the murky back side of the marijuana business—how coffeeshops get their supply from wholesalers. That's the "gray area" that Dutch laws have yet to sort out.

This esteemed coffeeshop, which works with the best boutique growers in Holland, regularly wins big at Amsterdam's annual Cannabis Cup Awards—a "high" honor, to be sure.

▶ *The next canal is...*

❺ Herengracht

Amsterdam added this canal during its Golden Age boom in the 1600s. It's named for the *heren,* the wealthy city merchants who lined it with their mansions. Even today, Herengracht runs through a high-rent district. (Zoning here forbids houseboats.)

Check out the house that's kitty-corner across the bridge, at Herengracht 150. It has features you'll find on many old Amsterdam buildings. On the roof, rods support the false-front gable. From this side view, you can see that, though a townhouse might have a narrow entrance, it can stretch far back from the street.

Notice the parking signs along Herengracht. Motorists have to put money in the meter at the end of the block or get towed. Parking is a major problem in a city like this.

▶ *Continue west, walking along...*

❻ Leliegracht

This is one of the city's prettiest small canals, lined with trees and

Leliegracht canal is short and sweet.

Herengracht—a canal of gabled townhouses

lanterns, and crossed by a series of arched bridges. There are some 400 such bridges in Amsterdam. It's a pleasant street of eccentric boutiques, trendy furniture shops, and bookstores. Notice that some buildings have staircases leading down below the street level to residences. Looking up, you'll see the characteristic beams jutting out from the top with a cargo-hoisting hook on the end. The view from a bay window here must be exceptional.

▶ *Continue on to the next canal, and pause on the* ❼ ***Keizersgracht Bridge***. *Take in another fine row of gables and the colorfully crowned tower of the Westerkerk—where we're headed. After the bridge, we'll take a detour off our westward route, and veer left along…*

❽ Keizersgracht

Walk south about 100 yards along the canal.

Homomonument: You'll reach a set of steps leading down to the water, where a triangular pink stone juts into the canal. This is part of the so-called Homomonument—a memorial to homosexuals who lost their lives in World War II, and a commemoration of all those persecuted for their sexuality. If you survey the square, you'll see that the pink triangle is just one corner of a larger triangle that comprises the entire Homomonument. (The pink-triangle design reclaims the symbol that the Nazis used to mark homosexuals.) You may see flowers or cards left here by friends and loved ones.

Westermarkt Square: Walk through the square called Westermarkt, between the church and busy Raadhuisstraat. You'll pass a pair of very Dutch kiosks. The first, called Pink Point, gives out information on gay and lesbian Amsterdam, especially nightlife. The next sells French fries; when it's closed, the shutters feature funny paintings putting *friets* into great masterpieces of Western art.

▶ *Keep walking toward the entrance to…*

❾ Westerkerk (Western Church)

Near the western end of the church, look for a cute little statue. It's of Anne Frank, who holed up with her family in a house just down the block from here.

Now, look up at the towering spire of the impressive Westerkerk. The crown shape was a gift of the Habsburg emperor, Maximilian I. In thanks for a big loan, the city got permission to use the Habsburg royal

A memorial to AIDS victims   The crown of the Westerkerk

symbol. The tower also displays the symbol of Amsterdam, with its three Xs. The Westerkerk was built in 1631, as the city was expanding out from Dam Square. Rembrandt's buried inside...but no one knows where. You can pop into the church for free or pay to climb to the tower balcony (just below the *XXX*) for a grand view (generally open May-Oct Mon-Sat 10:00-15:00, closed Sun, Nov-April closed Sat; for tower-climb details, see page 127).

The church tower has a carillon that chimes every 15 minutes. At other times, it plays full songs. Invented by Dutch bellmakers in the 1400s, a carillon is a set of bells of different sizes and pitches. There's a live musician inside the tower who plays a keyboard to make the music. Mozart, Vivaldi, and Bach—all of whom lived during the heyday of the carillon—wrote music that sounds great on this unique instrument. During World War II, the Westerkerk's carillon played every day. This hopeful sound reminded Anne Frank that there was, indeed, an outside world.

▶ *Continue around the church and walk north along the Prinsengracht canal to #263. This doorway was the original entrance to the...*

❿ Anne Frank House

This was where the Frank family hid from the Nazis for 25 months. With actual artifacts, the museum gives the cold, mind-boggling statistics of fascism the all-important intimacy of a young girl who lived through it and died from it. Even bah-humbug types find themselves caught up in Anne's story. ▭ See the Anne Frank House Tour chapter.

▶ *At the next bridge turn left. Stop at its summit, midcanal, for a view of...*

⓫ Prinsengracht

The "Princes' Canal" runs through what's considered one of the most livable areas in town. It's lined with houseboats, some of the city's estimated 2,500. These small vessels were once cargo ships—but by the 1930s, they had become obsolete. They found a new use as houseboats lining the canals of Amsterdam, where dry land is so limited and pricey.

Today, former cargo holds are fashioned into elegant, cozy living rooms. The once-powerful engines have generally been removed

A statue to Anne Frank remembers those who hid from the Nazis in the back of a nearby house.

to make more room for living space. Moorage spots are prized and grandfathered in, making some of the junky old boats worth more than you'd think. Houseboaters can plug hoses and cables into outlets along the canals to get water and electricity.

Notice the canal traffic. The official speed limit is about four miles per hour. At night, boats must have running lights on the top, the side, and the stern. Most boats are small and low, designed to glide under the city's bridges. The Prinsengracht bridge is average height, with less than seven feet of headroom (it varies with the water level); some bridges have less than six feet. Boaters need good charts to tell them the height, which is crucial for navigating. Police boats roam on the lookout for anyone CUI (cruising under the influence).

▶ *The recommended* **Café 't Smalle** *is a half-block to the right. Once you cross Prinsengracht, you enter what's officially considered the Jordaan neighborhood. Facing west (toward Café de Prins), cross the bridge and veer left down…*

⑫ Nieuwe Leliestraat

Welcome to the quiet Jordaan. Built in the 1600s as a working-class housing area, it's now home to artists and yuppies. The name Jordaan probably was not derived from the French *jardin*—but given the neighborhood's garden-like ambience, it seems like it should have been.

Train your ultra-sharp "traveler's eyes" on all the tiny details of Amsterdam life. Notice how the pragmatic Dutch deal with junk mail. On the doors, stickers next to mail slots say *Nee* or *Ja* (no or yes), telling the postman if they'll accept or refuse junk mail. Residents are allowed a "front-yard garden" as long as it's no more than one sidewalk tile wide. A speed bump in the road keeps things peaceful. The red metal bollards known as *Amsterdammertjes* ("little Amsterdammers") have been bashing balls since the 1970s, when they were put in to stop people from parking on the sidewalks. Though many apartments have windows right on the street, the neighbors don't stare and the residents don't care.

▶ *At the first intersection, turn right onto…*

⑬ Eerste Leliedwarsstraat

Pause and linger awhile on this tiny lane. Imagine the frustrations of home ownership here. If your house is considered "historic," you need special permission and lots of money to renovate.

On this street, you can see three different examples of renovation. At house #9, it was done cheap and dirty: A historic (but run-down) home was simply torn down and replaced with an inexpensive, functional building with modern heating and plumbing. At #5, there's no renovation at all. The owners were too poor (stuck with rent-control tenants), and they missed the window of time when a cheap rebuild was allowed. At #2A (across the street), the owners obviously had the cash to do a first-class sprucing up—it's historic-looking but fully modern inside. Even newly renovated homes like this must preserve their funky leaning angles and original wooden beams. They're certainly nice to look at, but absolutely maddening for owners who don't have a lot of money to meet city standards.

▶ *Just ahead, walk out to the middle of the bridge over the next canal (Egelantiersgracht). This is what I think of as...*

⓮ The Heart of the Jordaan

For me, this bridge and its surroundings capture the essence of the Jordaan. Take it all in: the bookstores, art galleries, working artists' studios, and small cafés full of rickety tables. The quiet canal is lined with trees and old, narrow buildings with gables—classic Amsterdam.

Looking south toward the Westerkerk, you'll see a completely different view of the church than most tourists get. Framed by narrow streets, crossed with streetlamp wires, and looming over shoppers on bicycles—to me, this is the church in its best light.

Turning around and looking north, you'll see the street called Tweede Egelantiersdwarsstraat—the laid-back Jordaan neighborhood's

Some residents live on houseboats.

Want junk mail? Tell the postman no or yes.

main shopping-and-people street. If you venture down there, you'll find boutiques, galleries, antique stores, hair salons, and an enticing array of restaurants.

▶ *Now head west along the canal (Egelantiersgracht) to the next bridge, where you'll turn left onto Tweede Leliedwarsstraat, and walk a few steps to #5.*

⓱ Electric Ladyland

This small shop, with a flowery window display, calls itself "The First Museum of Fluorescent Art." Its funky facade hides an illuminated wonderland within, with a tiny exhibit of black-light art. It's the creation of Nick Padalino—one cool cat who really found his niche in life. He enjoys personally demonstrating the fluorescence found in unexpected places—everything from minerals to stamps to candy to the tattoo on his arm. Wow (€5, by appointment only, required tours Wed-Sat at 14:00, 15:00, 16:00, and 17:00, closed Sun-Tue; www.electric-lady-land.com).

About 100 yards farther down the street and across the canal, old hippies might want to visit the **Paradox Coffeeshop.** It's the perfect

Nick welcomes you to his blacklight museum.

See no reefer, hear no reefer at Grey Area.   Jordaan's greatest sight: everyday life

coffeeshop for the nervous American who wants a friendly, mellow place to go local (see page 150).

▶ *To reach our last stop, backtrack 20 paces to the canal and turn left, then walk a few dozen yards to Egelantiersgracht #107, the entrance to...*

⑯ St. Andrew's Courtyard (Sint-Andrieshof)

The black door is marked *Sint-Andrieshof 107 t/m 145*. The doorway looks private, but it's the public entrance to a set of residences. It's generally open during daytime hours, except on Sundays. Enter quietly; you may have to push hard on the door. Go inside and continue through a blue-tile-lined passageway into a tiny garden courtyard (*hof*) surrounded by a dozen or so homes. Take a seat on a bench. This is one of the city's scores of similar *hofjes*—subsidized residences built around a courtyard, and funded by churches, charities, and the city for low-income widows and pensioners. This one, from 1613, is one of the oldest in Amsterdam.

▶ *And this is where our tour ends—in a tranquil world that seems right out of a painting by Vermeer. You're just blocks from the bustle of Amsterdam, but it feels like another world. You're immersed in the Jordaan, where everything's in its place, and life seems very good.*

Anne Frank House Tour

On May 10, 1940, Germany's Luftwaffe began bombing Schiphol Airport, preparing to invade the Netherlands. The Dutch army fought back, and the Nazis responded by leveling Rotterdam. Within a week, the Netherlands surrendered, Queen Wilhelmina fled to Britain, and Nazi soldiers goose-stepped past the Westerkerk and into Dam Square, where they draped huge swastikas on the Royal Palace. A five-year occupation began.

The Anne Frank House immerses you, in a very immediate way, in the struggles and pains of the war years. Walk through rooms where, for two years, eight Amsterdam Jews hid from Nazi persecution. Though they were eventually discovered, and all but one died in concentration camps, their story has an uplifting twist—the diary of Anne Frank, an affirmation of the human spirit that cannot be crushed.

ORIENTATION

Cost: €10.50, includes a good audioguide.

Hours: April-Oct daily 9:00-22:00; Nov-March Mon-Fri 9:00-20:00, Sat until 22:00, Sun until 19:00. Closed for Yom Kippur.

Information: Tel. 020/556-7105, www.annefrank.org.

Getting Tickets: The Anne Frank House is extremely popular and often sells out. Tickets are available online only. Even with a sightseeing pass you'll need to book an entrance time online (see next).

Reservations: Timed-entry tickets go on sale two months in advance (for example, to visit on Aug 15, you can buy online beginning June 15). Tickets are released gradually over a two-month period between the on-sale date and the visit date, with some tickets going on sale the day of. If no tickets for your preferred date are available initially, keep checking back.

Museumkaart holders get in free but must also reserve an entry time online for €0.50 (beginning two months in advance). You can make this reservation even if you haven't purchased a card yet—but be sure to buy the pass at another sight before your Anne Frank House visit.

Other Tips: If tickets are sold out for the day you want to visit, check the museum's website for last-minute tickets the evening before and the morning of your planned visit. Or book the "Introductory Program" (€15.50, includes museum entry, available about 2 months in advance). You'll hear a 30-minute talk (in English) about the rise of Nazism and the Frank family's struggles, then visit the museum on your own.

Getting There: It's at Prinsengracht 267, near Westerkerk and a 20-minute walk from Centraal Station. The museum entrance is around the corner, at Westermarkt 20. Or take tram #13 or #17—or bus #170, #172, or #174—to the Westermarkt stop.

What to Expect: You'll snake your way single file through the crowded museum. The house has many steep, narrow stairways that can be difficult for mobility-impaired visitors or the very young.

Length of This Tour: Allow one hour.

Baggage Check: Check coats and small bags. No large bags allowed.

Eating: The **$$** museum café serves simple fare and has good views.

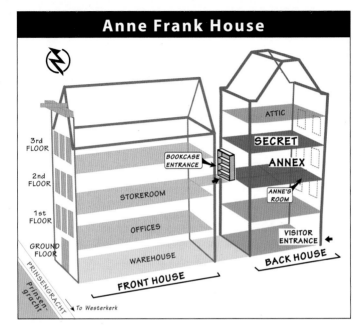

THE TOUR BEGINS

We'll walk through the rooms where Anne Frank, her parents, her sister, and four other Jews hid for 25 months. The front half of the building, facing the canal, remained the offices and warehouses of an operating business. The back half, where the Franks and others lived, was the Secret Annex, its entrance concealed by a swinging bookcase.

The museum recently went through a major renovation. The basic route should be as described here, but you'll also find new areas with more historical background. The good audioguide will lead you through any changes.

▶ *After the ticket desk, enter the ground-floor exhibit. Start with the important five-minute video. Then continue through a few more ground-floor rooms before going upstairs to the offices of the Franks' business.*

Otto Frank—Anne's father

Miep and Jan Gies helped the Franks hide.

First Floor: Offices

From these rooms, Otto Frank ran a successful business called Opekta, selling spices and pectin for making jelly. When the Nazis gained power in Germany in 1933, Otto moved his family from Frankfurt to tolerant Amsterdam, hoping for a better life.

Photos and displays bring to life the business concerns of Otto and his colleagues. During the Nazi occupation, while the Frank family hid in the back of the building, these brave people kept Otto's business running, secretly bringing supplies to the Franks. Miep Gies, Otto's secretary, brought food every few days, while bookkeeper Victor Kugler cheered up Anne with the latest movie magazines.

▶ Go upstairs to the...

Second Floor: Storeroom

Think of the circumstances that forced the Franks to move in here. As the Nazis swarmed over the Netherlands, they were at first lenient toward, even friendly with, the vanquished Dutch. But soon they began imposing restrictions that affected one in ten Amsterdammers—that is, Jews. Jews had to wear yellow-star patches and register with the police. They were banned from movie theaters and trams, and even forbidden to ride bikes.

In February 1941, the Nazis started rounding up Amsterdam's Jews, shipping them by train to "work camps," which, in reality, were transit stations on the way to death camps in the east. Outraged, the people of Amsterdam called a general strike that shut down the city for two days...but the Nazis responded with even harsher laws.

In July 1942, Anne's sister, Margot, got her **call-up notice** for a "work-force project." Otto could see where this was headed. He handed over the keys to the business to his "Aryan" colleagues, spread rumors that they were fleeing to Switzerland, and prepared his family to "dive under" (*onderduik,* as it was called) into hiding.

Photos put faces on the eight inhabitants of the Secret Annex. First was the Frank family—Otto and Edith and their daughters, 13-year-old Anne and 16-year-old Margot. A week later, they were joined by the Van Pels (called the "Van Daans" in her diary), with their teenage son, Peter. A few months later, Fritz Pfeffer (called "Mr. Dussel" in the diary) was invited in. **Videos** show interviews with Otto, Miep Gies, and Victor Kugler from the 1960s and '70s, describing how they organized the concealment, got supplies, and set up the Secret Annex.

▶ *At the back of the second floor storeroom is the clever hidden passageway into the Secret Annex, where eight people lived in a tiny apartment smaller than 1,000 square feet.*

Secret Annex

Though its furniture was ransacked during the arrest, the rooms of the annex remained virtually untouched, and we see them today much as they were.

The Bookcase Entrance

On a rainy Monday morning, July 6, 1942, the Frank family—wearing extra clothes to avoid carrying suspicious suitcases—breathed their last fresh air, took a long look at the Prinsengracht canal, and disappeared into the back part of the building, where they spent the next two years. Victor Kugler concealed the entrance to the annex with this swinging bookcase, stacked with business files.

Though not exactly a secret (since it's hard to hide an entire building), the annex was a typical back-house (*achterhuis*), a common feature in Amsterdam buildings, and the Nazis had no reason to suspect anything on the premises of the legitimate Opekta business.

▶ *Pass through the bookcase entrance into...*

Otto, Edith, and Margot's Room

The family carried on life as usual. Edith read from a **prayer book** in their native German, Otto read Dickens' ***Sketches by Boz,*** and the children continued their studies, with Margot taking **Latin lessons** by correspondence course. They avidly followed the course of the war through radio broadcasts and news from their helpers. As the tides of war slowly turned and it appeared they might one day be saved from the Nazis, Otto tracked the Allied advance on a **map** of Normandy.

The room is very small, even without the furniture. Imagine yourself and two fellow tourists confined here for two years.

Pencil lines on the wall track Margot's and Anne's heights, marking the point at which these growing lives were cut short.

Anne Frank's Room

Pan the room clockwise to see some of the young girl's idols in photos and clippings she pasted there herself: American stars Robert Stack and Deanna Durbin from the Cinderella-story film *First Love,* the future Queen Elizabeth II as a child, matinee idol Rudy Vallee, figure-skating actress Sonja Henie, and, on the other wall, actress Greta Garbo, actor Ray Milland, Renaissance man Leonardo da Vinci, and actress Ginger Rogers. Photos of flowers and landscapes gave Anne a window on the outside world she was forbidden to see.

Out the window (which had to be blacked out) is the back courtyard, which had a chestnut tree and a few buildings. (In 2010, the tree, which Anne had greatly enjoyed, toppled in a storm.) These things, along with the Westerkerk bell chiming every 15 minutes, represented the borders of Anne's "outside world." Imagine Anne sitting here at a small desk, writing in her diary.

In November 1942, the Franks invited a Jewish neighbor to join them, and Anne was forced to share the tiny room with Fritz Pfeffer, a middle-aged dentist.

The Bathroom

The eight inhabitants shared this bathroom. During the day, they didn't dare flush the toilet.

▶ *Ascend the steep staircase—silently—to the...*

Common Living Room

This was the kitchen (note the remains of the stove and sink) and dining room. Otto Frank was well off, and early on, the annex was well-stocked with food. Miep Gies would dutifully take their shopping list, buy food for her "family" of eight, and secretly lug it up to them. Buying such large quantities in a coupon-rationed economy was

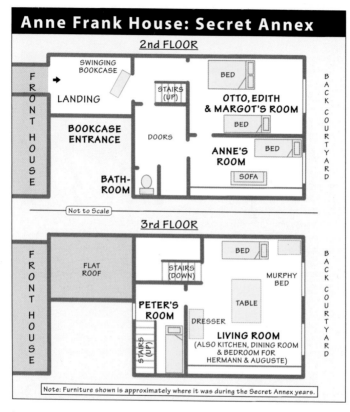

Anne Frank House: Secret Annex

2nd FLOOR

FRONT HOUSE

SWINGING BOOKCASE

LANDING

BOOKCASE ENTRANCE

DOORS

BATH-ROOM

STAIRS (UP)

BED

OTTO, EDITH & MARGOT'S ROOM

BED

ANNE'S ROOM

BED

SOFA

BACK COURTYARD

Not to Scale

3rd FLOOR

FRONT HOUSE

FLAT ROOF

STAIRS (DOWN)

PETER'S ROOM

DRESSER

STAIRS (UP)

BED

MURPHY BED

TABLE

LIVING ROOM (ALSO KITCHEN, DINING ROOM & BEDROOM FOR HERMANN & AUGUSTE)

BACK COURTYARD

Note: Furniture shown is approximately where it was during the Secret Annex years.

highly suspect, but she knew a sympathetic grocer (a block away on Leliegracht) who was part of a ring of Amsterdammers risking their lives to help the Jews.

The **menu** for a special dinner lists soup, roast beef, salad, potatoes, rice, dessert, and coffee. Later, as war and German restrictions plunged Holland into poverty and famine, they survived on canned foods and dried kidney beans.

The inhabitants spent their days reading and studying in this

Life in the Annex

By day, it's enforced silence, so no one can hear them in the offices. They whisper, tiptoe, and step around squeaky places in the floor. The windows are blacked out, so they can't even look outside. They read or study, and Anne writes in her diary.

At night and on weekends, when the offices close, one or two might sneak downstairs to listen to Winston Churchill's BBC broadcasts on the office radio. Everyone's spirits rise and sink with news of Allied victories and setbacks.

Anne's diaries make clear the tensions, petty quarrels, and domestic politics of eight people living under intense pressure. Mr. Van Pels annoys Anne, but he gets along well with Margot. Anne never gets used to Mr. Pfeffer, who is literally invading her space. Most troublesome of all, pubescent Anne often strikes sparks with her mom. (Anne's angriest comments about her mother were deleted from early editions of the published diary.)

Despite their hardships, the group feels guilty: They have shelter, while so many other Jews are being rounded up and sent off. As the war progresses, they endure long nights when the house shakes from Allied air raids, and Anne cuddles up in her dad's bed.

Boredom tinged with fear—the existentialist hell of living in hiding is captured so well in Anne's journal.

room. At night, it became sleeping quarters for Hermann and Auguste van Pels.

Peter van Pels' Room

On Peter's 16th birthday, he got a Monopoly-like board game called "The Broker" as a present. Initially, Anne was cool toward Peter, but after two years together, a courtship developed, and their flirtation culminated in a kiss.

The **staircase** (no visitor access) leads up to where the inhabitants stored their food. Anne loved to steal away here for a bit of privacy. At night they'd open a hatch to let in fresh air.

One hot August day, Otto was in this room helping Peter learn English, when they looked up to see a man with a gun. The hiding was over.

▶ *From here we leave the Secret Annex, returning to the Opekta storeroom and offices in the front house. As you work your way downstairs, you'll see a number of exhibits on the aftermath of this story.*

Aftermath

Arrest, Deportation, and Auschwitz Exhibits

On August 4, 1944, a German policeman accompanied by three Dutch Nazis pulled up in a car, politely entered the Opekta office, and went straight to the bookcase entrance. No one knows who tipped them off. The police gave the surprised hiders time to pack. They demanded their valuables and stuffed them into Anne's briefcase...after dumping her diaries onto the floor.

Taken in a van to Gestapo headquarters, the eight were processed in an efficient, bureaucratic manner, then placed on a train to Westerbork, a concentration camp northeast of the city. You'll see the **transport list,** which includes "Anneliese Frank," and their 3-by-5-inch **registration cards.**

From there they were locked in a car on a normal passenger train and sent to Auschwitz, a Nazi extermination camp in Poland. On the platform at Auschwitz, they were "forcibly separated from each other" (as Otto later reported) and sent to different camps. Anne and Margot were sent to Bergen-Belsen.

If it's playing, don't miss the **video** of one of Anne's former neighbors, Hannah Goslar, who ended up at Bergen-Belsen with Anne. In English she describes their reunion as they talked through a barbed-wire fence shortly before Anne died. She says of Anne, "She didn't have any more tears."

Anne and Margot both died of typhus in March 1945, only weeks before the camp was liberated. The other Secret Annex residents—except Otto—were gassed or died of disease.

The Franks' story was that of Holland's Jews. The seven who died were among the more than 100,000 Dutch Jews killed during the war years. (Before the war, 140,000 Jews lived in the Netherlands.) Of Anne's school class of 87 Jews, only 20 survived.

▶ *The next room is devoted to Anne's father.*

The Otto Frank Room

After the war, Otto returned to Amsterdam. Miep Gies had a gift for him—Anne's diaries, which she had found on the floor of the annex after the arrest. Listen to a 1967 **video,** in which Anne's father talks about his reaction as he read the diaries. He was struck by the enormous power of Anne's ideas and emotions—a secret world he'd never known inside his daughter. Determined to make her writings available to a wider audience, he set about contacting publishers (you may see his letters or notebooks or early typed-up drafts of the diaries). In 1947, the diaries were first published in Dutch as *De Achterhuis*—"The Back House."

▶ *Downstairs you come to...*

The Diaries

Anne wrote three diaries. (You may see one, two, or all three of them, as well as individual pages.) She received the first diary (with a red-plaid binding) as a birthday present when she turned 13, shortly before the family went into hiding. The other two were written in school-exercise books. Anne wrote the diaries in the form of a letter to an imaginary friend named Kitty.

As she wrote more and more, Anne began to recognize the uniqueness of her situation. You may see some loose-leaf pages on which she reworked parts of her diary. You may also see a book of Anne's short stories and a notebook she kept of favorite quotes.

When the diaries were published, the book quickly went viral. *De Achterhuis* in Dutch soon became *The Diary of a Young Girl* in English (1952), followed by translations in many other languages. The book became a popular play, *The Diary of Anne Frank,* and then a Hollywood movie.

▶ *Continue downstairs to the ground-floor exhibits.*

Anne's Legacy

These displays (which change often) capture the Anne Frank legacy.

You may see video interviews of people who knew Anne, such as

Anne's diaries chronicled both her tedious life in hiding and her expansive dreams.

childhood friends or Miep Gies (who passed away in 2010 at the age of 100). You may see memorabilia of the Franks and their friends (or even the Oscar statuette won by Shelley Winters for the 1959 movie). You may learn about Otto's struggles to save the house from demolition and turn it into a museum.

Otto wanted the Anne Frank House to be, in his words, "more than a museum." Its displays do not try to sum up "the moral" of the story. Instead, they recognize that World War II presented many gray areas and ethical dilemmas, and different people had different responses. The point? To keep visitors from leaving the museum with pat feelings of easy moral clarity.

The Anne Frank Foundation is obviously concerned that we learn from Europe's Nazi nightmare. The thinking that made the Holocaust possible still survives. Even today, some groups promote the notion that the Holocaust never occurred and contend that stories like Anne Frank's are only a hoax. It was Otto Frank's dream that visitors come away from the Anne Frank House with hope for a better world. He wrote: "The task that Anne entrusted to me continually gives me new strength to strive for reconciliation and for human rights all over the world."

Sights

Dynamic Amsterdam, laced with shimmering canals and lined with Golden-Age architecture, boasts magnificent museums, from the venerable Rijksmuseum (with Dutch Masters) to Van Gogh's starry collection to the thought-provoking Anne Frank House. The city has perhaps more specialty museums than any other city its size. From houseboats to sex, from marijuana to the Dutch resistance, you can find a museum to suit your interests.

The following sights are arranged by neighborhood for handy sightseeing. When you see a 📖 in a listing, it means the sight is covered in more depth in one of my walks or self-guided tours. A 🎧 means the walk or tour is available as a free audio tour (see page 11).

Remember that though the city has several must-see museums, its best attraction is its own carefree ambience.

Amsterdam Sights

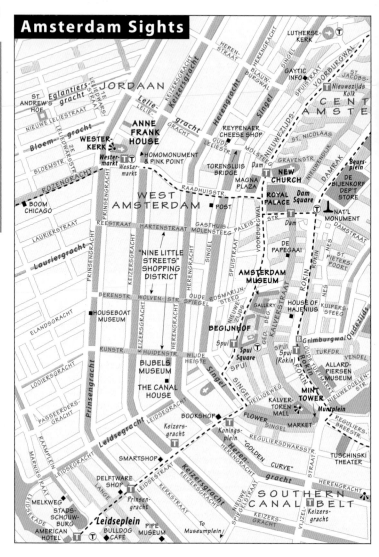

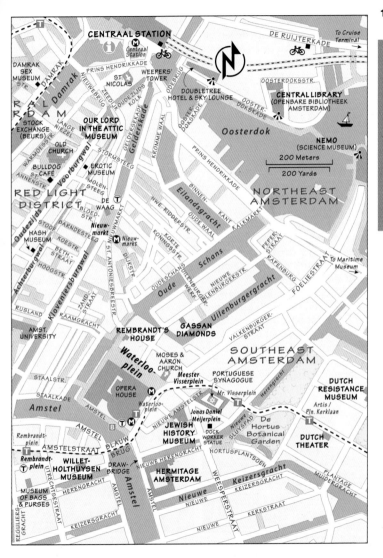

CENTRAAL STATION

DE RUIJTERKADE

To Cruise Terminal

Centraal Station

DAMRAK SEX MUSEUM

PRINS HENDRIKKADE

ST. NICOLAS

WEEPERS' TOWER

OOSTERDOKSSTR.

DOUBLETREE HOTEL & SKY LOUNGE

CENTRAL LIBRARY (OPENBARE BIBLIOTHEEK AMSTERDAM)

R A I L R D A M

STOCK EXCHANGE (BEURS)

OUR LORD IN THE ATTIC MUSEUM

OOSTER-DOKSKADE

Oosterdok

OLD CHURCH

PRINS HENDRIKKADE

NEMO (SCIENCE MUSEUM)

BULLDOG CAFÉ

EROTIC MUSEUM

200 Meters

200 Yards

RED LIGHT DISTRICT

DE WAAG

Nieuwmarkt

Eilandsgracht

BINNEN KANT

KALKMARKT

NORTHEAST AMSTERDAM

HASH MUSEUM

Nieuwmarkt

KORTE KONINGSSTR.

Schans

PEPER-STRAAT

RAPENBURG

To Maritime Museum

OUDESCHANS

NIEUWE UILENBURGERSTR.

Oude Waal

FOELIESTRAAT

Ullenburgergracht

AMST. UNIVERSITY

REMBRANDT'S HOUSE

GASSAN DIAMONDS

VALKENBURGER-STRAAT

SOUTHEAST AMSTERDAM

DUTCH RESISTANCE MUSEUM

Waterlooplein

MOSES & AARON CHURCH

Meester Visserplein

PORTUGUESE SYNAGOGUE

Mr. Visserplein

Artis / Pln. Kerklaan

OPERA HOUSE

Waterlooplein

Jonas Daniel Meijerplein

JEWISH HISTORY MUSEUM

De Hortus Botanical Garden

DUTCH THEATER

Amstel

DOCK WORKER STATUE

Rembrandt-plein

AMSTELSTRAAT

BLAUW BRUG

NIEUWE HERENGRACHT

HORTUSPLANTSOEN

Rembrandtplein

WILLET-HOLTHUYSEN MUSEUM

DRAW-BRIDGE

HERMITAGE AMSTERDAM

Keizersgracht

MUSEUM OF BAGS & PURSES

HERENGRACHT

Nieuwe

WEESPERSTRAAT

KERKSTRAAT

KEIZERSGRACHT

Advance Tickets and Sightseeing Passes

You should buy advance tickets online for the extremely popular Anne Frank House, Van Gogh Museum, and Rijksmuseum. Alternatively, a sightseeing pass lets you skip the ticket lines, though you still need to reserve an entrance time for the Anne Frank House and Van Gogh Museum. Entry to most sights is free with a sightseeing pass.

Advance Tickets: Buy tickets for the three major museums—Anne Frank House, Van Gogh Museum, and Rijksmuseum—through their websites; you can also buy advance tickets at TIs (though lines there can be long). Reservations for the Anne Frank House are extremely limited: Buy your ticket starting two months before the date of your visit (see page 106).

Museumkaart: This €60 sightseeing pass might be worthwhile for a short stay in the Netherlands, but can be a very good deal (with a little effort) for those staying longer. Buy the card at a participating museum (less crowded ones are the Royal Palace or New Church on Dam Square, or Amsterdam Museum a few blocks away). You'll get a **temporary card** that gives you five admissions, good for 31 days at around 400 museums across the country. In Amsterdam, if you visit the Rijksmuseum, Van Gogh Museum, Anne Frank House, and Amsterdam Museum, the pass just pays for itself. And, it lets you skip the ticket line at the Rijksmuseum.

You can upgrade your temporary card to a **one-year card** covering unlimited admissions by registering it online at www.museumkaart.nl/Registration. In a few days, a new one-year card is mailed to you. For a list of the 400 included museums, go to http://dutchmuseums.com/museumcard.php. I simply present my card at any Dutch museum to see if it's accepted.

You can wait in line for tickets… …or buy online in advance to guarantee entry.

The Museumkaart is sold at many participating museums. Buy it at a less crowded one to avoid lines. On Dam Square, get it at the Royal Palace or New Church, or at the Amsterdam Museum a few blocks away. Near Museumplein, buy it at the Stedelijk Museum or Coster Diamonds.

I Amsterdam City Card: Not as good a deal, the I Amsterdam City Card covers many Amsterdam sights (including a canal boat ride) and includes a transportation pass. It doesn't cover the Anne Frank House or museums outside of Amsterdam (€59/24 hours, €74/48 hours, €87/72 hours). A list of covered sights is at www.iamsterdamcard.com.

Other passes you'll see advertised, the **Holland Pass** and the **Amsterdam City Pass,** are not worth it.

Without Advance Tickets or a Pass: If you end up visiting the Anne Frank House without a reservation, trim your time in line by showing up late in the day; this works better in early spring and fall than in summer, when even after-dinner lines can be long. You can visit the Van Gogh Museum on weekend evenings until 21:00—with fewer lines or crowds—on Fridays year-round, and some Saturdays (July-Aug). For the Rijksmuseum and Van Gogh Museum, you may be able to buy same-day skip-the-line tickets at the Tours & Tickets shop on Museumplein and other locations around town.

Southwest Amsterdam

▲▲▲Rijksmuseum
The museum's incomparable collection of 17th-century Dutch Masters is led by Rembrandt's brooding canvases, Vermeer's slice-of-life moments, Hals' vivacious portraits, and Steen's whimsical tableaux.

📖 See the Rijksmuseum Tour chapter.

▲▲▲Van Gogh Museum
This remarkable museum features works by the troubled Dutch artist whose art seemed to mirror his life. Highlights include *Sunflowers, The Bedroom, The Potato Eaters,* and many brooding self-portraits.

📖 See the Van Gogh Museum Tour chapter.

▲▲Stedelijk Museum
The Netherlands' top modern-art museum is filled with a permanent collection of 20th-century classics as well as far-out, refreshing, cutting-edge temporary exhibits. This is a museum for exploring. You'll

Southwest Amsterdam

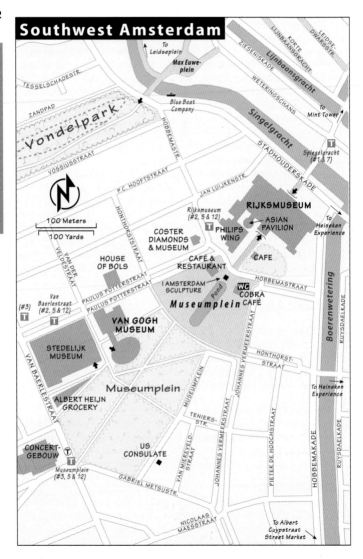

To Leidseplein

Max Euwe-plein

Blue Boat Company

LEIDSE-DWARSSTR.

KORTE LIJNBAANSGRACHT

LIJNBAANSGRACHT

ZIESENISKADE

Lijnbaansgracht

WETERINGSCHANS

TESSELSCHADESTR.

ZANDPAD

Vondelpark

Singelgracht

To Mint Tower

HOBBEMASTR.

STADHOUDERSKADE

Spiegelgracht (#1 & 7)

VOSSIUSSTRAAT

P.C. HOOFTSTRAAT

JAN LUIJKENSTR.

Rijksmuseum (#2, 5 & 12)

RIJKSMUSEUM

ASIAN PAVILION

100 Meters

100 Yards

HONTHORSTSTRAAT

COSTER DIAMONDS & MUSEUM

PHILIPS WING

To Heineken Experience

CAFÉ

VAN DER VELDESTRAAT

HOUSE OF BOLS

CAFÉ & RESTAURANT

HOBBEMASTRAAT

Van Baerlestraat (#2, 5 & 12) (#3)

PAULUS POTTERSTRAAT

PAULUS POTTERSTRAAT

I AMSTERDAM SCULPTURE

Pond

WC

COBRA CAFÉ

Museumplein

Boerenwetering

RUYSDAELKADE

VAN GOGH MUSEUM

STEDELIJK MUSEUM

HONTHORST-STRAAT

JOHANNES VERMEERSTRAAT

VAN BAERLESTRAAT

Museumplein

MUSEUMPLEIN

To Heineken Experience

ALBERT HEIJN GROCERY

CONCERT-GEBOUW

Museumplein (#3, 5 & 12)

US CONSULATE

TENIERS-STR.

VAN MIEREVELD-STRAAT

JOHANNES VERMEERSTRAAT

PIETER DE HOOCHSTRAAT

HOBBEMAKADE

RUYSDAELKADE

GABRIEL METSUSTR.

NICOLAAS MAESSTRAAT

To Albert Cuypstraat Street Market

Planning a Three-Museum Day

To see the Rijksmuseum, Van Gogh Museum, and Stedelijk Museum in a single day, there are two good strategies.

One approach is to see the museums chronologically, in historical order: First, Old Masters at the Rijksmuseum, then Impressionism at the Van Gogh, and finishing with modern art at the Stedelijk.

But if you're in town during the busy season, you can avoid crowds by following this plan: See the Van Gogh Museum right when it opens at 9:00, then visit the less-congested Stedelijk. From there, you could take in some extra sights (Coster Diamonds and the House of Bols on the Museumplein), and have lunch. Finally, hit the Rijksmuseum after 14:00, when crowds there begin to subside.

run across some famous works by Picasso, Chagall, and many more, but be sure to also pay special attention to the many Dutch artists who helped to create modern art.

▶ *€17.50, daily 10:00-18:00, Fri until 22:00, top-notch gift shop, Paulus Potterstraat 13, tram #2 or #12 from Centraal Station to Van Baerlestraat, tel. 020/573-2911, www.stedelijk.nl.*

▲**Museumplein**
Bordered by the Rijks, Van Gogh, and Stedelijk museums, and the Concertgebouw (classical music hall), this park-like square is interesting even to art haters. Amsterdam's best acoustics are found underneath the Rijksmuseum, where street musicians perform everything from chamber music to Mongolian throat singing. Mimes, human statues, and crafts booths dot the square, while locals enjoy a park bench. And the city's brilliant—and climbable—"I Amsterdam" marketing letters await the world's selfies.

Nearby is **Coster Diamonds,** a handy place to see a diamond-cutting and polishing demo (free, frequent, and interesting 30-minute tours followed by sales pitch, daily 9:00-17:00, Paulus Potterstraat 2, www.costerdiamonds.com). Their Diamond Museum is worthwhile only for those who have a Museumkaart (which covers entry) or feel the need to see even more diamonds (€10, daily 9:00-17:00, www.diamonds-amsterdam.com).

The **House of Bols: Cocktail & Genever Experience** is a

The Stedelijk has wild modern art.

Museumplein—a people-friendly park

self-guided walk through what is essentially an ad for Holland's leading distillery, culminating in a chance to taste local gins (€16, not covered by Museumkaart, daily 13:00-18:30, Fri-Sat until 21:00, last entry one hour before closing, must be 18, Paulus Potterstraat 14, www.houseofbols.com).

Heineken Experience

This famous brewery, having moved its operations to the suburbs, has converted its old headquarters into a slick, Disneyesque beerfest—with a beer-making simulation ride, do-it-yourself music videos, and plenty of hype about all things Heineken family and the quality of their beer. It's fun, if overpriced.

▶ *€18, €16 online, includes two drinks, daily 10:30-19:30, Fri-Sun until 21:00, longer hours July-Aug, last entry 2 hours before closing; tram #24 to Stadhouderskade; an easy walk from Rijksmuseum, Stadhouderskade 78, tel. 020/523-9222, www.heinekenexperience.com.*

▲Vondelpark

This huge, lively city park is popular with the Dutch—families with little kids, romantic couples, strolling seniors, and hipsters sharing blankets and beers. It's a favored venue for free summer concerts. On a sunny afternoon, it's a hedonistic scene that seems to say, "Parents...relax."

Southern Canal Belt

▲Leidseplein

Brimming with cafés, this people-watching mecca is an impromptu stage for street artists, accordionists, jugglers, and unicyclists. After dark, it hums.

Heineken brewery—a frothy "experience"

Vondelpark—paths, greenery, happy locals

For more on Leidseplein, see page 34 of the Amsterdam City Walk.

Rembrandtplein and Tuschinski Theater

One of the city's premier nightlife spots is the leafy Rembrandtplein (and the adjoining Thorbeckeplein). Rembrandt's statue stands here, along with a jaunty group of life-size statues giving us The Night Watch in 3-D. Several late-night dance clubs keep the area lively into the wee hours.

The nearby **Tuschinski Theater,** a movie palace from the 1920s (a half-block from Rembrandtplein down Reguliersbreestraat), glitters inside and out. The exterior forces the round peg of Art Nouveau into the square hole of Art Deco. Inside, the sumptuous decor features fancy carpets, slinky fixtures, and semi-abstract designs. Grab a seat in the lobby (free to enter) and watch the ceiling morph, or take one of their tours.

▸ *€13 for half-hour tour, daily 9:00-11:30, Reguliersbreestraat 26.*

▲Willet-Holthuysen Museum
(a.k.a. Herengracht Canal Mansion)

This 1687 townhouse is a must for devotees of Hummel-topped sugar bowls and Louis XVI-style wainscoting. For others, it's a pleasant look inside a typical (rich) home with much of the original furniture and decor. Forget the history and just browse through a dozen rooms of beautiful saccharine objects from the 19th century.

▸ *€10, Mon-Fri 10:00-17:00, Sat-Sun from 11:00, take tram #4 or #14 to Rembrandtplein and walk to Herengracht 605, tel. 020/523-1822, www.willetholthuysen.nl.*

The Dutch Made Holland

The word Nederland means "lowland." ("Holland" is just a nickname; North and South Holland are two of the country's 12 provinces.) The country occupies the delta near the mouth of three of Europe's large rivers, including the Rhine. In medieval times, inhabitants built a system of earthen dikes to protect their land from flooding caused by tides and storm surges. Much of the land of the Netherlands was reclaimed from the sea, rivers, and lakes.

Though only 8 percent of the Dutch labor force is made up of farmers, 70 percent of the land is cultivated: If you venture outside of Amsterdam, you'll travel through vast fields. Several Dutch icons originated directly from the country's unique landscape: Windmills and canals drained the land. Wooden shoes (klompen) allowed farmers to walk across soggy fields. (The shoes also float—making them easy to find should they come off in high water.) Tulips and other flowers grew well in the sandy soil near dunes. All this tinkering with nature prompted a popular local saying: "God made the Earth, but the Dutch made Holland."

Small Niche Museums

Museum of Bags and Purses (Tassenmuseum Hendrikje): This quirky-but-elegant collection crammed into a small 1664 canal house tells 500 years of bag and purse history (€12.50, daily 10:00-17:00, behind Rembrandtplein at Herengracht 573, tel. 020/524-6452, www.tassenmuseum.nl).

Pipe Museum (Pijpenkabinet): This unusual museum holds 300 years of pipes in a 17th-century canal house. The street-level shop, Smokiana, is almost interesting enough to be a museum itself (€10, Mon-Sat 12:00-18:00, closed Sun, tel. 020/421-1779, just off Leidsestraat at Prinsengracht 488, www.pijpenkabinet.nl).

The Canal House (Het Grachtenhuis): Though promoted as a way to experience a great canalside mansion, this is basically a series of empty rooms showing videos—interesting but pricey (€15, includes audioguide, Tue-Sun 10:00-17:00, closed Mon, Herrengracht 386, www.hetgrachtenhuis.nl).

West Amsterdam

The neighborhood around many of these sights is described in the 📖 Jordaan Walk chapter and 🎧 audio tour.

▲▲▲ Anne Frank House

Thirteen-year-old Anne and her family spent two years hiding in the back rooms of this townhouse during the Nazi occupation of World War II. The thoughtfully designed exhibit offers thorough coverage of the Frank family, Anne's diary, the stories of others who hid, and the Holocaust.

 📖 See the Anne Frank House Tour chapter.

Houseboat Museum (Woonbootmuseum)

In the 1930s, modern cargo ships came into widespread use—making small, sail-powered cargo boats obsolete. These little vessels found new life as houseboats lining the canals of Amsterdam. Today, 2,500 such boats—their cargo holds turned into classy, comfortable living rooms—are called home. For a peek into this *gezellig* (cozy) world, visit this tiny museum. Captain Vincent enjoys showing visitors around his 100-year-old houseboat, which feels lived-in because, until 1997, it was.

▶ *€4.50; daily 10:00-17:00 except closed Mon Sept-June; on Prinsengracht, opposite #296 facing Elandsgracht, tel. 020/427-0750, www.houseboatmuseum.nl.*

Westerkerk

This landmark Protestant church has a barren interior, Rembrandt's body buried somewhere under the pews, and Amsterdam's tallest steeple with a grand view. The Westerkerk tower is climbable only

Anne Frank House—now a museum

Houseboat Museum with Captain Vincent

with a guided 30-minute tour (limited to six people; reserve in person on the same day or call).

▶ *Church entry—free, generally Mon-Sat 10:00-15:00, closed Sun, Nov-April closed Sat-Sun, Prinsengracht 281, tel. 020/624-7766, www. westerkerk.nl; tower—€7.50, by tour only, Mon-Sat 10:00-20:00, closed Sun and Nov-March, tours leave on the half-hour, http://www. westertorenamsterdam.nl.*

Central Amsterdam, near Dam Square

The following sights are included in my 📖 Amsterdam City Walk chapter and 🎧 audio tour.

▲Royal Palace (Koninklijk Huis)

Built as a lavish City Hall (1648-1655)—when Holland was a proud new republic and Amsterdam was the richest city on the planet—this building became a "Royal Palace" when Napoleon installed his brother Louis as king (1806). Subsequently it became the home of the Dutch royal family (the House of Orange). And today, it's one of King Willem-Alexander's official residences. About 20 lavishly decorated rooms are open to the public.

The highlight is the vast, white **Citizens' Hall**—120 feet by 60 feet by 90 feet, and lit by eight big chandeliers. At the far end, a statue of Atlas holds the globe of the world, and the ceiling painting shows Lady Amsterdam triumphant amid the clouds of heaven. On the floor, inlaid maps show the known world circa 1750 (back when the West Coast of the US was still being explored). The hall is used today to host foreign dignitaries and for royal family wedding receptions.

You'll also see the room where Louis Bonaparte's throne once sat (in front of the fireplace), a room of impressive Empire Style furniture (high-polished wood with Neoclassical motifs), and the childhood bedroom of former Queen Beatrix. The palace's rich chandeliers, paintings, statues, and furniture reflect Amsterdam's historic status as the center of global trade.

▶ *€10, includes good audioguide, daily 10:00-17:00 but hours can vary for official business—check website, tel. 020/522-6161, www. paleisamsterdam.nl.*

New Church (Nieuwe Kerk)

Barely newer than the Red Light District's "Old" Church, this

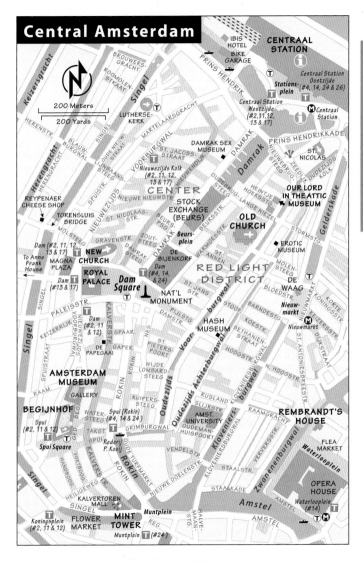

Central Amsterdam

SIGHTS

IBIS HOTEL
BIKE GARAGE
CENTRAAL STATION
Centraal Station Oostzijde (#4, 14, 24 & 26)
Stationsplein
Centraal Station Westzijde (#2, 11, 12, 13 & 17)
Centraal Station

200 Meters
200 Yards

BROUWERSGRACHT
ROOMOLENSTRAAT
PRINS HENDRIK
PRINS HENDRIKKADE

Keizersgracht
Singel
HERENSTR.
LUTHERSEKERK
MARTELAARSGRACHT
Herengracht
HERENGRACHT
BLAUWBURGWAL
OUDE NIEUW
VOORBURGWAL
ST. JACOBSSTRAAT
DAMRAK SEX MUSEUM
Damrak
ST. NICOLAS
ZEEDIJK
OUDEZIJDS KOLK
NIEUWEBRUG STEEG

Nieuwezijds Kolk (#2, 11, 12, 13 & 17)
CENTER
NIEUWENDIJK
HEINTJE HOEKSTEEG
OUDEBRUG STEEG-LANGE NIEZEL
OUR LORD IN THE ATTIC MUSEUM

REYPENAER CHEESE SHOP
ST. NICOLAASSTR.
NIEUWE NIEUWSTR.
STOCK EXCHANGE (BEURS)
BEURSSTR.
WARMOESSTR.
OLD CHURCH
STORMSTG.
Gelderskade

TORENSLUIS BRIDGE
SPUISTR.
MOLSTEEG
GRAVENSTR.
ZOUTSTEEG
Beursplein
ST. ANNEN
EROTIC MUSEUM

Dam (#2, 11, 12, 13 & 17)
To Anne Frank House
MAGNA PLAZA
NEW CHURCH
DAMRAKSTEEG
DE BIJENKORF
RED LIGHT DISTRICT
MOLENSTEEG
DE WAAG
KORTE KONINGSTR.

Dam (#13 & 17)
ROYAL PALACE
Dam Square
Dam (#4, 14, & 24)
ST. JANSSTR.
ST. JANSburgwal
STOOF
BLOEDSTR.
Nieuwmarkt
KEIZERSSTR.
KONINGSSTR.

PALEISSTR.
NAT'L MONUMENT
PIJLSTG.
DAMSTR.
BARNDESTG.
Nieuwmarkt
ST. ANTONIESBREESTR.
DIJKSTRAAT

Singel
KEIZERRIJK
NIEUWEZIJDS VOORBURGWAL
Dam (#2, 11 & 12)
SPAAR
NES
ST. PIETERSPOORT
HASH MUSEUM
KOESTR.
BETHANIENSTRAAT
HOOGSTRAAT
N. HOOGSTR.

AMSTERDAM MUSEUM
DE PAPEGAAI
GAPER
WIJDE LOMBARDSTEEG
Voorburgwal
Oudezijds Achterburgwal
KLOVENIERSBURGWAL
REMBRANDT'S HOUSE

GALLERY
ROKIN
ROKIN
KUIPERSTEEG
RUSLAND
AMST. UNIVERSITY
RAAMGRACHT
FLEA MARKET

BEGIJNHOF
Spui (#2, 11 & 12)
WATERSTEEG
Spui (Rokin) (#4, 14 & 24)
SLIJKSTR.
OUDEMANHUISPOORT
KLOVENIERSBURGWAL
VERVERSSTR.
Waterlooplein

Spui Square
GEDEMTAKSTR.
GRIMBURGWAL
Rederij P. Kooij
OUDE TURFMARKT
VENDELSTR.
STAALSTR.
OPERA HOUSE
Waterlooplein (#14)

KALVERSTR. K.
ROKIN
NIEUWE DOELENSTR.
KLOVENIERSBURGWAL
STAALKADE
Amstel

HEILIGEWEG K.
KALVERTOREN MALL
SINGEL
FLOWER MARKET
MINT TOWER
Muntplein
REG.
MAY HAV STG.
AMSTEL
Koningsplein (#2, 11 & 12)
Muntplein (#24)

15th-century sanctuary has a spare interior, lots of tradition (many Dutch royal weddings and coronations), and popular temporary exhibits.

▶ *Free to view from gift-shop balcony, interior with special exhibits—€9-16, daily 10:00-17:00, audioguide-€4 or free depending on exhibit, on Dam Square, tel. 020/638-6909, www.nieuwekerk.nl.*

▲▲Amsterdam Museum

This creative museum traces the city's growth from fishing village to world trade center to hippie haven. Start with the easy-to-follow "DNA" section, which hits the historic highlights from 1000-2000. Then try not to get lost somewhere in the 17th century as you navigate the meandering maze of rooms. The museum's free pedestrian corridor—called the Amsterdam Gallery and lined with old-time group portraits—is a powerful teaser.

▶ *€15, free for kids 17 and under, includes audioguide, daily 10:00-17:00, pleasant restaurant in courtyard before entrance, mandatory and free bag check, next to Begijnhof at Kalverstraat 92, tel. 020/523-1822, www.amsterdammuseum.nl.*

▲Begijnhof

Stepping into this tiny, idyllic courtyard in the city center, you escape into the charm of old Amsterdam.

See page 28 of the Amsterdam City Walk chapter.

▲▲Our Lord in the Attic Museum
(Museum Ons' Lieve Heer op Solder)

For two centuries (1578-1795), Catholicism in Amsterdam was illegal but tolerated. When hard-line Protestants took power in 1578, Catholic churches were vandalized and shut down. The city's Catholics gathered secretly to say Mass in homes and offices. In 1663, a wealthy merchant built Our Lord in the Attic (Ons' Lieve Heer op Solder), one of a handful of places in Amsterdam that served as a secret parish church until Catholics were once again allowed to worship in public.

The church was hidden within the businessman's own home. From the outside, it's a typical townhouse on a historic canal. But within lies a 150-seat, three-story church that's the size of a four-lane bowling alley. The museum's one-way route will take you through living spaces in the front of the townhouse, then the secret church, and finally the "back house" (*achterhuis,* a common feature in historic townhouses).

▶ *€11, includes audioguide, Mon-Sat 10:00-18:00, Sun from 13:00, Oudezijds Voorburgwal 38, tel. 020/624-6604, www.opsolder.nl.*

▲▲Red Light District Walk

Europe's most popular ladies of the night tease and tempt here, as they have for centuries, in streets surrounding the historic Old Church (Oude Kerk). The neighborhood also boasts sex shops, sex museums, marijuana cafes, and a marijuana museum. It's liveliest and least seedy in the early evening.

◻ See the Red Light District Walk chapter.

Sex Museums

Amsterdam has three sex museums. While visiting one can be called sightseeing, visiting more than that is harder to explain.

The cheapest and most interesting is the **Damrak Sex Museum,** which tells the story of pornography from Roman times through 1960. Every sexual deviation is revealed: early French pornographic photos; memorabilia from Europe, India, and Asia; a Marilyn Monroe tribute; and some S&M displays (€5, not covered by Museumkaart, daily 9:30-23:00, Damrak 18, a block in front of Centraal Station, tel. 020/622-8376, www.sexmuseumamsterdam.nl).

The **Erotic Museum** is five floors of uninspired paintings, videos, old photos, and sculpture (€7, not covered by Museumkaart, daily 11:00-24:00, along the canal at Oudezijds Achterburgwal 54, tel. 020/624-7303, www.erotisch-museum.nl).

Red Light Secrets Museum of Prostitution is a pricey look at the world's oldest profession. If you're wondering what it's like to sit in

The historic Our Lord in the Attic house has... ...a hidden Catholic church in the attic.

those red booths, watch the video taken from the prostitute's perspective as "johns" check you out (€12.50, €9.50 online, not covered by Museumkaart, daily 10:00-24:00, Oudezijds Achterburgwal 60, tel. 020/662-5300, www.redlightsecrets.com).

Northeast Amsterdam

Central Library (Openbare Bibliotheek Amsterdam)

This huge, striking, multistory building holds almost 1,400 seats—many with wraparound views of the city. Everything's relaxed and inviting, from the fun kids' zone and international magazine and newspaper section on the ground floor to the organic cafeteria, with its dramatic view-terrace restaurant on the top. The library is a 10-minute walk from the east end of Centraal Station.

▶ *Free, daily 10:00-22:00, tel. 020/523-0900, www.oba.nl.*

NEMO Science Museum

This kid-friendly science museum is a city landmark, with its distinctive copper-green building, jutting up from the water like a sinking ship.

Exhibits, permanent and rotating, allow kids (and adults) to explore science by playing with bubbles and giant dominoes, or doing simple experiments. Up top is a restaurant with a great city view.

▶ *€16.50, free for kids 3 and under, daily 10:00-17:30 except closed Mon Sept-mid-Feb, tel. 020/531-3233, www.nemosciencemuseum.nl. The roof terrace—open until 20:00 in the summer—is generally free. From Centraal Station, you can walk there in 15 minutes, or take bus #22 or #48 to the Kadijksplein stop.*

▲▲Netherlands Maritime Museum
(Nederlands Scheepvaartmuseum)

Given the Dutch seafaring heritage, this is an appropriately important and impressive place. The east building holds the core collection: globes, an exhibit on the city's busy shipping port, original navigational tools, displays of ship ornamentation, and paintings of dramatic 17th-century naval battles against the British. The west building has exhibits on whaling and of seafaring in the Dutch Golden Age.

Moored outside is a replica of the *Amsterdam,* an 18th-century

NEMO's ship-shape science museum

Go below decks at the Maritime Museum.

cargo ship of the Dutch East India Company. Wander the decks, then duck your head and check out the captain and surgeon's quarters and the hold. The ship is light on good historical information, but ship-shape enough to delight history buffs. The **Royal Barge** next door is no replica. Built for King William I in the early 19th century, this gaudy boat was purely ceremonial—a symbol of House of Orange might.

▶ *€16, €7.50 for kids 5-17, includes audioguide, daily 9:00-17:00, bus #22 or #48 from Centraal Station to Kattenburgerplein 1, tel. 020/523-2222, www.scheepvaartmuseum.nl.*

North Amsterdam

▲EYE Film Institute Netherlands

The most striking feature of the Amsterdam skyline is EYE, a film museum and cinema housed in an übersleek modern building immediately across the water from Centraal Station. The complex includes museum spaces and theaters for art films, special exhibits, a shop, and a trendy terrace café with great waterside seating.

▶ *General entry and basement exhibit are free, fee for films and exhibits; open 10:00-19:00, cinemas open daily at 10:00 until last screening, tel. 020/589-1400, www.eyefilm.nl. From the docks behind Centraal Station, catch the free ferry (labeled Buiksloterweg) across the river and walk left to the big white modern building.*

Southeast Amsterdam

Waterlooplein Flea Market

For more than a hundred years, the Jewish Quarter flea market has raged daily except Sunday (at the Waterlooplein Metro station, behind Rembrandt's House). The long, narrow park is filled with stalls selling cheap clothes, hippie stuff, old records, and tourist knickknacks.

▲Rembrandt's House (Museum Het Rembrandthuis)

A middle-aged Rembrandt lived here from 1639 to 1658 after his wife's death, as his popularity and wealth dwindled down to obscurity and bankruptcy. As you enter, ask when the next etching or painting demonstration is scheduled and pick up the excellent audioguide.

During your visit, you'll explore Rembrandt's reconstructed house, filled with period objects that duplicate what his bankruptcy inventory of 1656 said he owned. Imagine him at work in his studio. Marvel at his personal collection of exotic objects, many of which he included in paintings. Attend an etching demonstration to learn about drawing in soft wax on a metal plate that's then dipped in acid, inked up, and printed. For the finale, enjoy several rooms dedicated (generally) to original Rembrandt etchings. You're not likely to see a single Rembrandt painting in the whole house, but this interesting museum may make you come away wanting to know more about the man and his art.

▸ *€13, includes audioguide, daily 10:00-18:00, etching and paint-making demonstrations almost hourly, Jodenbreestraat 4, tel. 020/520-0400, www.rembrandthuis.nl.*

Gassan Diamonds

Many shops in this "city of diamonds" offer tours. Here you'll see experts behind magnifying glasses polishing the facets of precious diamonds, followed by a visit to an intimate sales room to see (and perhaps buy) a mighty shiny yet very tiny souvenir.

▸ *Free, daily 9:00-17:00, Nieuwe Uilenburgerstraat 173, tel. 020/622-5333, www.gassan.com.*

▲▲Hermitage Amsterdam

The famous Hermitage Museum in St. Petersburg, Russia loans art to Amsterdam for a series of rotating special exhibits in the Amstelhof, a huge 17th-century building along the Amstel River.

By law, the great Russian collection can only be out of the country for six months at a time, so the exhibit is always changing (check

Rembrandt's House has a modern entrance.

Gassan's free diamond-polishing demo

the museum's website to see what's on display). One small permanent exhibit explains the historic connection between the Dutch (Orange) and Russian (Romanov) royal families.

▶ *Generally €17.50, discount with Museumkaart, daily 10:00-17:00, audioguide-€4, mandatory free bag check, café, Nieuwe Herengracht 14, tram #14 from Centraal Station, tel. 020/530-7488, www.hermitage.nl.*

De Hortus Botanical Garden

An oasis of tranquility within the city, this large park is one of the oldest botanical gardens in the world, from 1638. As Dutch sailors and botanists roamed the globe, they returned with medicinal herbs, cacti, tropical palms, and the first coffee plant in Europe.

▶ *€9.50, not covered by Museumkaart, daily 10:00-17:00, inviting café, Plantage Middenlaan 2A, tel. 020/625-9021, www.dehortus.nl.*

▲Jewish Historical Museum (Joods Historisch Museum) and Portuguese Synagogue

A single ticket admits you to these two sights, located a half-block apart. The Jewish Historical Museum tells the story of the Netherlands' Jews through three centuries. The collection spreads across four historic former synagogues that have been joined by steel and glass to make one modern complex.

Start in the impressive **Great Synagogue.** Have a seat and picture it during its prime (1671-1943): men worshipping downstairs, women above in the gallery. On the east wall (the symbolic direction of Jerusalem) is the alcove where they keep the scrolls of the Torah. The raised platform in the center of the room is where the text was sung.

Video displays around the room explain Jewish customs, from birth (circumcision) to puberty (the bar/bat mitzvah, celebrating the entry into adulthood) to Passover celebrations to marriage.

Next, head upstairs where exhibits trace the history of Amsterdam's Jews from 1600 to 1900. Exhibits about Jews in the 20th century are housed in the former **New Synagogue.** Personal artifacts—chairs, clothes—tell the devastating story of the Holocaust in a very real way.

Finish your visit across the street at the **Portuguese Synagogue.** Built in the 1670s, the majestic, spacious place of worship survived World War II, though its congregation barely did.

A Torah at the Jewish Historical Museum   Dutch Theater, where Nazis imprisoned Jews

▶ *€15, also covers Dutch Theater/National Holocaust Memorial; museum open daily 11:00-17:00; Portuguese Synagogue Sat-Thu 10:00-17:00, Fri until 15:00 or 16:00, free audioguide, café; take tram #14 to Mr. Visserplein, Jonas Daniel Meijerplein 2; tel. 020/531-0310, www.jhm.nl.*

▲Dutch Theater (Hollandsche Schouwburg), a.k.a. National Holocaust Memorial

Once a lively theater in the Jewish neighborhood, and today a moving memorial, this building was used as an assembly hall for local Jews destined for Nazi concentration camps. On the wall, 6,700 family names pay tribute to the 107,000 Jews deported and killed by the Nazis. Some 70,000 victims spent time here, awaiting transfer.

Upstairs is a dated-but-evocative history exhibit with a model of the ghetto, plus photos and memorabilia (such as shoes and letters), putting a human face on the staggering numbers. Back in the ground-floor courtyard, notice the hopeful messages that visiting school groups attach to wooden tulips.

▶ *Donation requested, free with Jewish Historical Museum/Portuguese Synagogue ticket, daily 11:00-17:00, take tram #14 to Artis, Plantage Middenlaan 24, tel. 020/531-0380, www.hollandscheschouwburg.nl.*

▲▲Dutch Resistance Museum (Verzetsmuseum)

Bam—it's May 1940 and the Germans invade the Netherlands, destroy Rotterdam, drive Queen Wilhelmina into exile, and—in four short days of fighting—hammer home the message that resistance is futile.

This museum tells the rest of the story of how the Dutch survived under Nazi occupation from 1940 to 1945. They faced a timeless moral dilemma: Is it better to collaborate with a wicked system to effect small-scale change—or to resist outright, even if your efforts are doomed to fail? You'll learn why some chose the former, and others the latter.

You'll see propaganda movie clips, study forged ID cards under a magnifying glass, and read about ingenious and courageous efforts—big and small—to undermine the Nazi regime. Vandals turned Nazi V-for-Victory posters into W-for-Wilhelmina. Printers circulated underground newspapers. Farmers organized a milk strike. Ordinary citizens hid radios under floorboards and Jews inside closets. They suffered through the "Hunger Winter" of 1944 to 1945, during which 20,000 died. Finally, it was springtime, the Allies liberated the country, and Nazi helmets were turned into Dutch bedpans.

▶ €11, €6 for kids 7-15, includes audioguide; Mon-Fri 10:00-17:00, Sat-Sun from 11:00, mandatory free bag check, tram #14 from the train station or Dam Square, Plantage Kerklaan 61, tel. 020/620-2535, www.verzetsmuseum.org.

▲Tropical Museum (Tropenmuseum)

As close to the Third World as you'll get without lots of vaccinations, this imaginative museum offers wonderful re-creations of tropical life and explanations of Third World problems (largely created by Dutch colonialism and the slave trade). Ride the elevator to the top floor, and circle your way down through this immense collection, opened in 1926 to give the Dutch people a peek at their vast colonial holdings.

▶ €15, €8 for kids 4-18, daily 10:00-17:00, closed Mon off-season, café, tram #14 to Linnaeusstraat 2, tel. 020/568-8200, www.tropenmuseum.nl.

Day Trips

The Netherlands' efficient train system turns much of the country into a feasible day trip. The Dutch have done away with paper tickets for domestic trains; instead travelers use smartcards (part of the "OV-chipkaart system") that can be bought at ticket machines and counters. If you're taking just three or four train trips in the Netherlands, buy a "single-use chipcard"—a paper ticket that contains a chip—each time you travel. You can only purchase these single-use tickets on the day you are traveling, and you'll pay a €1 surcharge per ticket. So, for a day trip from Amsterdam to Haarlem, you'll pay €8 for a round-trip ticket, plus the €1 surcharge.

▲▲Haarlem

A half-hour away by train, the town of Haarlem is an agreeable mix of quaintness, history, and contemporary Dutch life.

The center of town is the massive main church, the **Grote Kerk.** Inside the church is Holland's largest organ (5,000 pipes) plus quirky exhibits like a replica of Foucault's pendulum and a 400-year-old cannonball. A spacious square **(Grote Markt)** surrounds the church. Sip a coffee or beer at one of the cafés, and take in a view that's looked much the same for 700 years and been captured in well-known paintings. The square hosts colorful market days on Monday (clothing) and Saturday (general).

Haarlem is the hometown of Frans Hals, and the **Frans Hals Museum** has the world's largest collection of his work. Stand eye-to-eye with life-size, lifelike, warts-and-all portraits of Golden Age brewers, preachers, workers, bureaucrats, and housewives. Most impressive are Hals' monumental group portraits.

The **Teylers Museum,** the Netherlands' oldest, almost feels like a museum of a museum, with its well-preserved exhibits of fossils, minerals, and primitive electronic gadgetry.

In Haarlem, the main church anchors a town that's both quaint and contemporary.

The **Corrie ten Boom House** relates the inspirational story of a family that courageously hid Jews from the Nazis. Finally (two blocks northeast of Grote Markt, off Lange Begijnestraat), you can stroll through quaint Haarlem's cozy little **Red Light District.**

▶ *Trains to Haarlem depart Amsterdam's Centraal Station several times an hour. From Haarlem's train station, the town center is a 10-minute walk—ask a local to point you to the "Grote Markt." There's a bike rental in the station. Avoid Haarlem on Mondays when many sights are closed. Haarlem's friendly TI (VVV) is in the Town Hall building on Grote Markt (tel. 023/531-7325, www.haarlem.nl).*

▲Other Dutch Destinations

The charming, canal-laced town of **Delft** (hometown of Vermeer and blue-painted ceramics) and its neighbor city, **The Hague** (famous for its Old Masters in the Maurithuis Gallery), make a rewarding day or two of sightseeing. **Arnhem** has the Netherlands Open-Air Museum and the Kröller-Müller Museum of Van Gogh paintings (in Hogue Veluwe National Park). The **Historic Triangle** offers a nostalgic loop trip on a steam train and boat. **Keukenhof's** flower garden is one of the world's best (open in spring only). College-town **Leiden** is the Netherlands' answer to Cambridge or Oxford, while mighty **Rotterdam**—whose core and port were bombed flat during World War II—now is Europe's busiest port with a gleaming modern skyline. Medieval **Utrecht** is known for its lively downtown core and Holland's top railway museum.

If you want more, there's also **Edam** (an adorable village), **Alkmaar** (best on Friday for its cheese market), **Aalsmeer** (a bustling modern flower auction), **Schokland** (for a chance to walk on what was the bottom of the sea at this village/museum), and open-air folk museums at **Enkhuizen** and **Zaanse Schans.**

For more info on these places visit www.holland.com.

Activities

Amsterdam offers much more than famous museums. Consider a floating introduction to the city on a guided canal boat tour (some people prefer to cruise at night, when Amsterdam's bridges are illuminated). Explore Amsterdam's history, architecture, Red Light District, or food scene with a group or private walking tour. You can even pedal around the city with a guided bike tour, or rent a bike and follow my "do-it-yourself" tour.

To round out your experiences, go on a shopping blitz, spend an evening at the theater or a concert, roll with the locals on skate night, or—for those so inclined—enjoy an "herbal" experience at a traditional "coffeeshop" (a café selling marijuana).

TOURS

Traditional Canal Boat Tours

These long, low, tourist-laden boats leave continually from several docks around town for a relaxing, if uninspiring, one-hour introduction to the city (with recorded headphone commentary), worth ▲▲. Select a boat tour based on your proximity to its starting point. The I Amsterdam City Card covers the Blue Boat Company and Gray Line boats. Tip: Boats leave only when full, so jump on a full boat to avoid waiting at the dock.

Rederij P. Kooij is cheapest (€11; boats docking opposite Centraal Station go 2-3/hour daily 10:00-16:00; boats docking off Rokin 125 go 3/hour in summer 10:00-22:00, 2/hour in winter 10:00-17:00; tel. 020/623-3810, www.rederijkooij.nl).

Blue Boat Company's boats depart from near Leidseplein (€18, €16 if you book online; daily 10:00-18:00, every half-hour March-Oct, hourly Nov-Feb 10:00-18:00; 1.25 hours, Stadhouderskade 30, tel. 020/679-1370, www.blueboat.nl).

Gray Line-Stromma offers a one-hour trip and longer tours from the docks opposite Centraal Station (€18, €15 online, one-hour "100 Highlights" tour, daily 2-4/hour 9:00-21:00; Prins Hendrikkade 33a, tel. 020/217-0500, www.stromma.nl).

Smaller, Quirkier Canal Boat Tours

They are youthful, come with hip narration, encourage drinking, and are simply lots of fun.

Those Dam Boat Guys gives 1.5-hour tours with entertaining and knowledgable guides (generally ex-pats who ask for tips). They encourage you to bring a picnic (or drinks, or joints) and make a party of it (€25, not meant for younger kids, meet at Café Wester on corner of Nieuwe Leliestraat and Prinsengracht, tel. 06-1885-5219, sign up online at www.thosedamboatguys.com).

Friendship Amsterdam Boat Tours offers more standard one-hour tours in open boats seating about 40 (€15, 3/hour daily between 10:00 and noon, Oudezijds Voorburgwal 230 in Red Light District, tel. 020/334-4774, www.friendshipamsterdam.com).

Red Light District Tours

Randy Roy's Red Light Tours consists of one expat American woman, Kimberley. She gives fun, casual yet informative 1.5-hour walks through this neighborhood. Call, email, or send a WhatsApp message to reserve (€17.50 includes a drink, nightly at 20:00, no tours Dec-Feb, meet in front of Victoria Hotel—in front of Centraal Station, mobile 06-4185-3288, www.randyroysredlighttours.com).

Food Tours

Eating Amsterdam takes 8-12 people on an eight-stop, four-hour food tour of the Jordaan neighborhood. You'll sample cheese, cider, pancakes, *bitterballen,* herring, apple pie, and more (€79, Tue-Sat at 11:00; food tour with canal boat-€106, Tue–Sat at 10:30; tel. 020/808-3099, www.eatingamsterdamtours.com, Camilla Lundberg).

City Walking Tours

Free City Walk: New Europe Tours "employs" native English-speaking students to give irreverent and entertaining three-hour walks. This long walk covers a lot of the city with an enthusiasm for the contemporary pot-and-prostitution scene (free but tips expected, 5/day, www.neweuropetours.eu). All tours leave from the National Monument on Dam Square.

Private Guides: Larae Malooly and her team offer lively cultural and historic tours, with the option to join a small group or upgrade to a private tour tailored to your interests (€35 small group tours up to 10 people, €175 private tours for up to 4 people, www.amsterdamsel.com).

Albert Walet is a knowledgeable local guide who enjoys personalizing tours for Americans interested in getting to know his city (€70/2 hours, €120/4 hours, up to 4 people, on foot or by bike, mobile 06-2069-7882, abwalet2@yahoo.nl).

Dennis from Love My City Tours offers a customized introduction

Private guides nourish your knowledge.

Guided bike tours cover lots of ground.

Do-It-Yourself Bike Tour of Amsterdam

For a good day-trip enjoying bridges, bike lanes, and sleepy, off-the-beaten-path canals, rent a bike at or near Centraal Station and try this route: Head west down Haarlem-merstraat, working your wide-eyed way down Prinsengracht (drop into Café 't Papeneiland at Prinsengracht 2) and de-touring through the small, gentrified streets of the Jordaan neighborhood before popping out at the Westerkerk under the tallest spire in the city.

Pedal south to the lush and peaceful Vondelpark, then cut back through the center of town (Leidseplein to the Mint Tower, along Rokin street to Dam Square). From there, cruise the Red Light District, following Oudezijds Voorburgwal past the Old Church (Oude Kerk) to Zeedijk street, and return to the train station.

Then, you can escape into the countryside by hopping on the free ferry behind Centraal Station. In five minutes, Amsterdam is gone, and you're rolling through your very own Dutch painting.

to the city's neighborhoods plus great tips for places to eat and experiences not found on the tourist route (from €25/person for small groups up to 10, private tours from €100, mobile 06-3840-2919, www.lovemy-citytours.com, support@lovemycitytours.com).

Guided Bike Tours

Yellow Bike Guided Tours offers city bike tours of two hours or three hours, plus a four-hour, 15-mile tour of the dikes and countryside (reservations smart, tel. 020/620-6940, www.yellowbike.nl).

Joy Ride Bike Tours offers group tours designed to show you all of the clichés—cheese, windmills, and clogs—as you pedal through the pastoral polder land in 4.5 hours (mobile 06-4361-1798, www.joyridetours.nl).

SHOPPING

Amsterdam brings out the browser even in those who were not born to shop. The city has lots of one-of-a-kind specialty stores, street markets, and specific streets and neighborhoods worthy of a browse. For information on shopping, pick up the TI's *Shopping in Amsterdam* brochure.

Souvenir Ideas: You won't need a guidebook to find plenty of shops selling wooden shoes, blue-and-white Delftware (ranging from inexpensive fireplace titles to very expensive antiques), *jenever* (Dutch gin made from juniper berries, sold in traditional stone bottles), chocolate (Verkade or Droste cocoa in tins), or flower seeds and bulbs (be sure they're US Customs-friendly).

Department Stores

Hema is handy for everything from inexpensive clothes and notebooks to cosmetics. Stores are at Kalverstraat 212, in the Kalvertoren shopping mall, and at Centraal Station (both open daily). The **De Bijenkorf** department store, towering high above Dam Square, is Amsterdam's top-end option. The entire fifth floor is a ritzy self-service cafeteria with a rooftop terrace (store open daily).

Open-Air Markets

Amsterdam's biggest open-air market, **Albert Cuyp,** stretching for several blocks along Albert Cuypstraat, bustles from roughly 9:00-17:00 every day except Sunday. You'll find fish, exotic vegetables, bolts of fabric, bargain clothes, native Dutch and ethnic food stands. It's a 10-minute walk east of Museumplein and a block south of the Heineken Experience (tram #24).

While flower shops are scattered around the city, the most enjoyable browsing is at the **Flower Market,** which stretches luxuriously along the Singel canal between the Mint Tower and Koningsplein. The **Waterlooplein flea market** (daily except Sun near Waterlooplein Metro station) has stalls of garage-sale junk/treasure.

Top Shopping Zones

The city's top shopping areas are all equally good, but each has a different flavor.

The **Nine Little Streets** (De Negen Straatjes) are touristy, tidy, and central—hemmed in by a grid plan between Dam Square and the

Albert Cuyp market—shop till you drop.   Enjoy classical music at various venues.

Jordaan. The area is home to a diverse array of shops mixing festive, inventive, nostalgic, practical, and artistic items. For a preview, see www.theninestreets.com.

Haarlemmerstraat/Haarlemmerdijk, the area just west of Centraal Station, has morphed from a bit grotty into a thriving and trendy string of shops, cafés, and restaurants. A browse here is a fun chance to spot new trends, and maybe to pick up some local clothes and goods (vintage and casual young fashions abound).

The lively street called **Staalstraat** boasts more than its share of creative design shops. It's tucked in a youthful area just east of the university zone, and while it's good for shopping, it's also wonderful just for a relaxing stroll. **The Jordaan** is a mellow residential zone with a smattering of fine shops and the busy Noordermarkt market.

VAT and Customs

Getting a VAT Refund: If you purchase more than €50 worth of goods at a single store, you may be eligible to get a refund of the 21 percent Value-Added Tax (VAT). Get more details from your merchant or see www.ricksteves.com/vat.

Customs for American Shoppers: You can take home $800 worth of items per person duty-free, once every 31 days. You can bring in one liter of alcohol duty-free. For details on allowable goods, customs rules, and duty rates, visit http://help.cbp.gov.

NIGHTLIFE

Many Amsterdam hotels serve breakfast until 11:00 because so many people—visitors and locals—live for nighttime in this city.

On summer evenings, people flock to the main squares for drinks at outdoor tables. Leidseplein is the liveliest square, surrounded by theaters, restaurants, and nightclubs. The slightly quieter Rembrandtplein (with adjoining Thorbeckeplein and nearby Reguliersdwarsstraat) is the center of gay clubs and nightlife. Spui features a full city block of bars. The Red Light District (particularly Oudezijds Achterburgwal) is less sleazy, even festive, in the early evening (before 22:30).

The TI's website, www.iamsterdam.com, has good English listings for upcoming events. Newsstands sell the *A-Mag* entertainment guide, and the free cultural magazine *Uitkrant* is available at TIs, bars, and bookstores.

Music

Classical Music: You'll find free classical music at the **Concertgebouw** at far south end of Museumplein (tel. 0900-671-8345, www.concertgebouw.nl). For chamber music and contemporary works, visit the **Muziekgebouw aan 't IJ,** a mod concert hall on the waterfront, near the train station (Piet Heinkade 1, tel. 020/788-2000, www.muziekgebouw.nl). For opera and dance, try the **opera house** in the Stopera building (Amstel 3, tel. 020/625-5455, www.operaballet.nl). In the summer, Vondelpark hosts open-air concerts.

Also in summer, the **Westerkerk** has free lunchtime concerts most Fridays at 13:00 (May-Oct), plus an annual Bach organ concert cycle in August (Prinsengracht 281, tel. 020/624-7766, www.westerkerk.nl). The **New Church** offers periodic organ concerts and a religious music festival in June (Dam Square, tel. 020/626-8168, www.nieuwekerk.nl). The Red Light District's **Old Church** (Oude Kerk) has carillon concerts Tuesday and Saturday at 16:00 (Oudekerksplein 23, tel. 020/625-8284, www.oudekerk.nl).

Jazz: Jazz has a long tradition at the **Bimhuis** nightclub, housed in a black box jutting out from the Muziekgebouw performance hall, right on the waterfront. Its great bar has citywide views and is open to the public after concerts (Piet Heinkade 3, tel. 020/788-2188, www.bimhuis.com).

Rock and Hip-Hop: The beat goes on at these two clubs, just off Leidseplein: **Paradiso** (Weteringschans 6, tel. 020/626-4521, www.paradiso.nl) and **Melkweg** (Lijnbaansgracht 234a, tel. 020/531-8181, www.melkweg.nl). Both present big-name acts that you might recognize...if you're younger than me.

Comedy and Theater

Boom Chicago: This R-rated comedy improv act (in English) has been entertaining tourists and locals for years with rude, clever, and high-energy sketches mixed with improv games. If you need a break from museums and canal boat tours, this might be the ticket (€22-27, no shows Mon, in the Jordaan a couple of long blocks past Westerkerk at Rozengracht 117, tel. 020/217-0400, www.boomchicago.nl).

Theater: Amsterdam is one of the world centers for experimental live theater (much of it in English). Many theaters cluster around the street called the Nes, which stretches south from Dam Square. You can browse the offerings on the theaters' websites: **Vlaams Cultuurhuis de Brakke Grond** (www.brakkegrond.nl), **Frascati** (www.frascatitheater.nl), and **Tobacco Theater** (www.tobacco.nl).

Other Late-Night Fun

Movies: In the Netherlands most movies are subtitled, so English-only speakers have plenty of cinematic options. It's not unusual for movies at many cinemas to be sold out—consider buying tickets in advance. Catch a movie at the classic 1920s **Tuschinski Theater** (see page 125) or the splashy **EYE Film Institute Netherlands** (see page 133).

Museums Open Late: The **Anne Frank House** is open daily until 22:00 from April to October and Saturdays until 22:00 in the off-season. The **Stedelijk Museum's** collection of modern art is on view until 22:00 on Fridays. The **Van Gogh Museum** is open until 21:00 on Fridays year-round (when it sometimes has music and a wine bar in the lobby), and on Saturdays in July and August. Amsterdam's **marijuana** and **sex museums** stay open until at least 22:00.

Skating After Dark: Amsterdammers get their skating fix every Friday night in Vondelpark. Huge groups don in-line skates and meet at the round bench near the Vondel Pavilion (around 20:15, www.fridaynightskate.com). Anyone can join in. Ask your hotelier about the nearest place to rent skates, or try SkateDoktor (www.skatedokter.nl).

Tuschinski Theater, a 1920s movie palace

Pot's on the menu at coffeeshops.

MARIJUANA (CANNABIS)

For tourists from lands where you can do hard time for lighting up, the open use of marijuana here can feel either somewhat disturbing, or exhilaratingly liberating...or maybe just normal. Several decades after being decriminalized in the Netherlands, marijuana causes about as much excitement here as a bottle of beer.

Marijuana Laws and "Coffeeshops"

Throughout the Netherlands, you'll see "coffeeshops"—cafés selling marijuana, with display cases showing various joints or baggies for sale. The retail sale of marijuana is strictly regulated, and proceeds are taxed. The minimum age for purchase is 18, and coffeeshops can sell up to five grams of marijuana per person per day. It's also illegal for these shops (or anyone) to advertise marijuana. In fact, in many places, the prospective customer must take the initiative and ask to see the menu.

Shops sell marijuana and hashish both in pre-rolled joints and in little baggies. Joints are generally sold individually (€4-5, depending on whether it's hash with tobacco, marijuana with tobacco, or pure marijuana), though some places sell only small packs of three or four joints. Baggies generally contain a gram and go for €8-15.

Smoking Tips

Shops have loaner bongs and inhalers, and dispense rolling papers like toothpicks. While it's good style to ask first, if you're a paying customer (e.g., you buy a cup of coffee), you can generally pop into any coffeeshop and light up, even if you didn't buy your pot there.

Don't ever buy pot on the street in Amsterdam. Well-established coffeeshops are considered much safer, and coffeeshop owners have an interest in keeping their trade safe and healthy.

The Dutch sell several forms of cannabis: They smoke both hashish (an extract of the cannabis plant) and the leaf of the plant (which they call "marihuana" or "grass"). While hash is mostly imported from Morocco, most of the marijuana sold in Dutch coffeeshops is grown locally, as coffeeshops find it's safer to deal with Dutch-grown plants than to import marijuana (the EU prohibits any international drug trade).

"Coffeeshops" in Amsterdam

Most of downtown Amsterdam's coffeeshops feel grungy and foreboding to American travelers who aren't part of the youth-hostel crowd. I've listed a few places with a more pub-like ambience for Americans wanting to go local, but within reason. Most purchases are in cash.

Paradox is the most *gezellig* (cozy), a mellow, graceful place whose staff are patient with descriptions and happy to walk you through all your options (two blocks from Anne Frank House at Eerste Bloemdwarsstraat 2, tel. 020/623-5639, www.paradoxcoffeeshop.com). **The Grey Area**—a hole-in-the-wall spot with three tiny tables—is a cool, welcoming place appreciated among local aficionados as a perennial winner at Amsterdam's Cannabis Cup Awards (between Dam Square and Anne Frank House at Oude Leliestraat 2, tel. 020/420-4301, www.greyarea.nl). The flagship branch of the touristy **Bulldog Café coffeeshop** chain is in a former police station right on Leidseplein, offering alcohol upstairs and pot downstairs (Leidseplein 17, tel. 020/625-6278, www.thebulldog.com).

Sleeping

I've grouped my hotel listings into four neighborhoods: **West Amsterdam** (quiet canals, charming gabled buildings), **Central Amsterdam** (shopping and tourist sights, though a bit gritty), the **Southern Canal Belt** (restaurants and nightlife while still cozy), and **Southwest Amsterdam** (a semi-suburban neighborhood around Vondelpark and Museumplein).

I like hotels that are clean, central, reasonably priced, friendly, small enough to have a hands-on owner and stable staff, and run with a respect for Dutch traditions.

Book as far in advance as possible. Amsterdam is jammed during tulip season (late March-mid-May), conventions, festivals, summer weekends, and some national holidays.

Amsterdam Hotels

Amsterdam is a tough city for budget accommodations, and any hotel room under €150 (or B&B room under €125) will have rough edges. Still, you can sleep well and safely in a great location for around €100 per double. Canalside rooms can come with great views—and early-morning construction-crew noise. Light sleepers should ask for a quiet room in the back.

Canal houses were built tight. They have steep stairs with narrow treads, and only some have elevators. If that's a problem, look for a hotel with an elevator—and confirm that it reaches your room.

Breakfast—sometimes included in the room price—is normally a self-service buffet of fresh bread, cereal, ham, cheese, yogurt, juice, and coffee or tea.

Making Reservations

Reserve your rooms as soon as you've pinned down your travel dates. Book your room directly via email or a phone call, or through the hotel's official website. The hotelier wants to know:

- Type(s) of rooms you want and size of your party
- Number of nights you'll stay
- Your arrival and departure dates, written European-style as day/month/year (18/06/20 or 18 June 2020)
- Special requests (en suite bathroom, cheapest room, twin beds vs. double bed, quiet room)
- Applicable discounts (such as a Rick Steves reader discount, cash discount, or promotional rate)

Most places will request a credit-card number to hold your room. If you book direct, you can email, call, or fax this information. If you must cancel, it's courteous—and smart—to do so with as much notice as possible. Cancellation policies can be strict; read the fine print. Always call to reconfirm your reservation a few days in advance. For B&Bs or very small hotels, I call again on my day of arrival to tell my host what time I expect to get there (especially if arriving after 17:00).

Budget Tips

Comparison shop by checking prices at several hotels (on each hotel's own website, on a booking site, or by email). For the best deal, *book directly with the hotel*. Ask for a discount if paying in cash; if the listing

Sleep Code

Dollar signs reflect average rates for a standard double room with breakfast in high season.

$$$$	**Splurge:** Most rooms €200
$$$	**Pricier:** €150–200
$$	**Moderate:** €100–150
$	**Budget:** €50–100
¢	**Backpacker:** Under €50
RS%	**Rick Steves discount**

Unless otherwise noted, credit cards are accepted, hotel staff speak basic English, and free Wi-Fi is available.

includes **RS%,** request a Rick Steves discount. Some hotels extend a discount to those who pay cash or stay longer than three nights. Ask for details when you reserve.

If you're staying four or more nights, it's worth considering an apartment or rental house. These can be especially cost-effective for groups and families. European apartments, like hotel rooms, tend to be small by US standards. But they often come with laundry machines and small, equipped kitchens, making it easier and cheaper to dine in. Websites such as Airbnb, FlipKey, Booking.com, VRBO, and VacationRentals let you browse properties and correspond directly with European property owners or managers.

Amsterdam's traditional B&Bs offer you a chance to feel like a local while paying less than you would for a hotel room. Unfortunately, traditional B&Bs may be an endangered species in Amsterdam, where AirBnB is controversial and the city is clamping down on short-term rentals in homes. Some of my long-term listings have scaled back, and a few have closed entirely. If you enjoy getting to know the Dutch and appreciate a personal touch, stay at one before it's too late.

WEST AMSTERDAM

Tree-lined canals, gabled buildings, and candlelit restaurants; just minutes on foot to Dam Square. Many of my hotels are old mansions—charming but with lots of steep stairs.

$$$$ The Toren Chandeliered mansion, pleasant canalside setting, peaceful garden, classy yet friendly, on quiet street, RS%, breakfast extra, air-con, elevator.

Keizersgracht 164, tel. 020/622-6033, www.thetoren.nl

$$$$ Hotel Ambassade Elegant, traditional, and modern; staff is top-notch, RS%, breakfast extra, air-con, elevator, some stairs.

Herengracht 341, tel. 020/555-0222, www.ambassade-hotel.nl

$$$$ 't Hotel Cozy 17th-century house, fresh rooms, garden and canal views, tea room, family room, air-con.

Leliegracht 18, tel. 020/422-2741, www.thotel.nl

$$$$ Suites Aan de Singel by Vera Splurge B&B, two sophisticated rooms overlooking canal, one with a separate luxury bath, fans.

Singel 374, mobile 06-4595-7459, www.suitesaandesingel.nl

$$$ The Times Hotel Business-comfort hotel, scenic canal setting, tight modern rooms—some have bathtubs, breakfast extra, air-con, elevator.

Herengracht 135, tel. 020/330-6030, www.thetimeshotel.com

$$$ Wiechmann Hotel Spacious but worn, sparsely furnished rooms, cozy public area oozes Old World charm, lots of stairs, no elevator, some canal views, back rooms quiet.

Prinsengracht 328, tel. 020/626-3321, www.hotelwiechmann.nl

$$$ Hotel Brouwer Woody and old-time homey, tranquil yet central location, canal views, some rough edges, small elevator.

Singel 83, tel. 020/624-6358, www.hotelbrouwer.nl

$$$ Hotel Hegra Cozy, 17th-century merchant's house overlooking the canal, clean and modern, some rooms are small, some canal views, breakfast extra.

Herengracht 269, tel. 020/623-7877, www.hotelhegra.nl

$$$ Max Brown Hotel Trendy urban design geared toward hipsters, quiet neighborhood, modern rooms and public areas, continental breakfast, tangled floor plan connects three canalside buildings.

Herengracht 13, tel. 020/522-2345, www.maxbrownhotels.com

$$$ Mr. Jordaan Hotel In Greenwich Village-like neighborhood, funky-but-stylish rooms, some very tight, RS%—use "enjoyjordaan" when booking, breakfast extra, elevator.

Bloemgracht 102, tel. 020/626 5801, www.mrjordaan.nl

$$$ Linden Hotel Mr. Jordaan sister hotel, similar decor, tight rooms, slightly cheaper, some canal views, RS%—use "enjoylinden" when booking, family rooms, fans, breakfast extra.

Lindengracht 251, 020/622-1460, www.lindenhotel.nl

$$$ Herengracht 21 B&B Two stylish, intimate rooms in canal house filled with art, lovely host, air-con, private tours offered in 1920s canal boat.

Herengracht 21, tel. 020/625-6305, www.herengracht21.nl

$$ Hotel Hoksbergen Budget option for a canalside setting, cramped rooms, lived-in feel, bathrooms up to snuff, steep stairs, avoid cramped Room 4, ask about apartments, fans.

Singel 301, tel. 020/626-6043, www.hotelhoksbergen.com

$$ Truelove Guesthouse Room-rental service with rooms and apartments sprinkled throughout the Jordaan, stylish apartments come with kitchens and pull-out beds, no breakfast.

Prinsenstraat 4, mobile 06-5334-0866, info@trueloveguesthouse.com

¢ The Shelter Jordan Christian-run, great neighborhood, drug- and alcohol-free, men on one floor and women on another, Amsterdam's best budget beds, hot meals, Bible study.

Bloemstraat 179, tel. 020/624-4717, www.shelter.nl

CENTRAL AMSTERDAM

Ideal for shopping, tourist sights, and public transportation, but the area has traffic noise and urban grittiness, and the hotels can lack character.

$$$ Hotel Ibis Amsterdam Centre Next to Centraal Station, modern and efficient, comfort and value without a hint of charm, breakfast extra, book well in advance, air-con, elevators.

Stationsplein 49, tel. 020/721-9172, www.ibishotel.com

$$$ Hotel Résidence Le Coin Larger-than-average rooms with small kitchenettes, rooms appear slightly dated, breakfast extra, elevator.

Nieuwe Doelenstraat 5, tel. 020/524-6800, www.lecoin.nl

$$$ Hotel Nes Well-located boutique hotel, books up six months in advance, rooms tight but modish, some with canal views, elevator, breakfast extra.

Kloveniersburgwal 137, tel. 020/624-4773, www.hotelnes.com

¢ The Shelter City In the heart of the Red Light District, well-run and perfectly safe, drug- and alcohol-free, men on one floor and women on another, hot meals, Bible study.

Barndesteeg 21, tel. 020/625-3230, www.shelter.nl

SOUTHERN CANAL BELT

Mom-and-pop B&B-style coziness within a five-minute walk of restaurants and rowdy nightlife. Walk or easy tram to the center of town or Museumplein.

$$$ Hotel de Leydsche Hof Hidden gem on a canal, four large rooms with tree-filled backyard or canal views, lots of stairs, elegant old building.

Leidsegracht 14, tel. 020/638-2327, www.hoteldeleydschehof.com

$$$ Wildervanck B&B Two tastefully decorated rooms in elegant 17th-century canal house, run by friendly Dutch family, cash only, breakfast in pleasant dining room.

Keizersgracht 498, tel. 020/623-3846, www.wildervanck.com

SOUTHWEST AMSTERDAM

Semi-suburban neighborhood within walking distance of Vondelpark and Museumplein. Good-value modern accommodations (elevators) but less Old World charm.

$$$ Hotel Piet Hein Stylishly sleek yet comfortable rooms, swanky lounge, peaceful garden, on a quiet street, "economy double" seriously tight, good breakfast extra, air-con.

Vossiusstraat 51, tel. 020/662-7205, www.hotelpiethein.nl

$$$ Hotel Fita Bright rooms close to Van Gogh Museum, modern yet rustic, well-run, espresso machines in every room, air-con in some, elevator, free laundry service.

Jan Luijkenstraat 37, tel. 020/679-0976, www.fita.nl

$$ Hotel Alexander Modern hotel on a quiet street; smart, clean, relaxed place; garden patio, breakfast extra, elevator, some stairs.

Vondelstraat 44, tel. 020/589-4020, www.hotelalexander.nl

$$ Bed & Breakfast Amsterdam Three cozy rooms—some on a canal, clean and bright, cheaper room with shared bath, cash only, milk-and-cereal breakfast, no shoes, not many stairs.

Sloterkade 65, tel. 020/679-2753, www.bedandbreakfastamsterdam.net

$ Hotel Parkzicht Old-fashioned, no-frills place, extremely steep stairs, big and somewhat frayed rooms, books up quickly, cheaper rooms with shared bath, no elevator, some noise.

Roemer Visscherstraat 33, tel. 020/618-1954, www.parkzicht.nl

¢ Stayokay Vondelpark (IYHF) One of Amsterdam's top hostels, feels comfortable for all ages, some doubles, family rooms, lots of school groups, bike rental, right on Vondelpark.

Zandpad 5, tel. 020/589-8996, www.stayokay.com

Eating

Amsterdam's thousand-plus eateries make for a buffet of dining options. Choose from elegant candlelit restaurants, an exotic Indonesian *rijsttafel,* a light meal outdoors alongside a canal, herring at a fish stand, or takeout "Flemish" fries with mayonnaise. Besides meals, the Dutch spend endless hours sitting and drinking at outdoor cafés. Budget some money—and time—to sightseeing for your palate.

My listings are in Amsterdam's atmospheric neighborhoods, handy to recommended hotels and sights. Most are in Central Amsterdam (around Dam Square, Spui, and the Mint Tower), West Amsterdam (near the Anne Frank House and the Jordaan—the most charming place to dine), and Southwest Amsterdam (close to the museum quarter).

No matter where you dine, expect it to be *gezellig*—a much-prized Dutch virtue, meaning an atmosphere of relaxed coziness.

Restaurant Code

Dollar signs reflect the cost of a typical main course.

$$$$	**Splurge:**	Most main courses over €30
$$$	**Pricier:**	€20-30
$$	**Moderate:**	€10-20
$	**Budget:**	Under €10

A *friets* stand or other takeout spot is **$**; a basic café or sit-down eatery is **$$**; a casual but more upscale restaurant is **$$$**; and a swanky splurge is **$$$$**.

When in Amsterdam...

When in Amsterdam, I eat on the Dutch schedule. For breakfast, I eat at the hotel (bread, meat, cheese, eggs) or grab a pastry and coffee at a café. Lunch (12:00-14:00) is a simple sandwich (*broodje*) or soup. In between meals, I might stop at a takeout stand for French fries (*friets*) or a pickled herring. In the late afternoon, Amsterdammers enjoy a beverage with friends at an outdoor table on a lively square. Dinner (18:00-21:00) is the biggest meal of the day, the time for slowing down and savoring a multicourse restaurant meal.

Restaurants

As English is spoken everywhere, and the Dutch take an elegant-but-casual approach to dining, there's no need to learn a lot of special Dutch etiquette. At Dutch restaurants that have waitstaff, 15 percent service is included in the menu price, although it's common to round up the bill after a good meal (usually 5-10 percent). The Dutch are willing to pay for bottled water with their meal (Spa brand is popular, sparkling or still), but free tap water is always available upon request.

Cafés and Bars

Besides full-service restaurants, there are other places to fill the tank.

A café or eetcafé is a simple restaurant serving basic soups, salads, and sandwiches, as well as traditional meat-and-potatoes meals in a generally comfortable but no-nonsense setting. A *salon de thé* serves tea and coffee, but also pastries and sandwiches. At night, cafes are essentially "bars," catering to the drinking crowd.

Bruin cafés ("brown cafés") are named for their nicotine-stained walls—until smoking was banned indoors in 2008, they were filled with tobacco smoke. They are usually more bar-like, with dimmer lighting and wood paneling. A *proeflokaal* is a bar (with snacks) offering wine, spirits, or beer. A "coffeeshop" is a café where marijuana is sold and consumed, though most offer drinks and munchies, too.

Cafés and bars with outdoor tables generally charge the same whether you sit inside or out. When ordering drinks in a café or bar, you can just pay as you go (especially if the bar is crowded), or wait until the end to settle up, as many locals do. If you get table service, take the cue from your waiter. There's no need to tip if you order at the counter, but if you get table service, it's nice to round up to the next euro ("keep the change").

Most cafés have a light-fare menu of sandwiches, salads, and soups, but some offer more ambitious meals. Throughout the day they cater to customers who just want to relax over a drink.

The Dutch love their coffee, enjoying many of the same drinks (espresso, cappuccino) served in American or Italian coffee shops.

Most cafés and bars won't charge you more for dining outdoors.

Eat, drink, and be merry on city squares.

Herring sandwich—what's not to love?

A *koffie verkeerd* (fer-KEERT, "coffee wrong") is an espresso with a lot of steamed milk. Many cafés/bars have a juicer for making fresh-squeezed orange juice, and they'll have the full array of soft drinks.

Order "a beer," and you'll get a *pils*—a light pilsner-type beer in a 10-ounce glass with a thick head leveled off with a stick. Typical brands are Heineken, Grolsch, Oranjeboom, Amstel, and the misnamed Bavaria (brewed in Holland). Belgian beers are also popular.

The Dutch enjoy a chilled shot of *jenever* (yah-NAY-ver), a Dutch gin made from juniper berries. *Jong* (young) is sharper; *oude* (old) is mellow and more expensive. You'll find a variety of local fruit brandies and cognacs. The Dutch people drink a lot of fine wine, but it's almost all imported.

Picnicking

Amsterdam makes it easy to turn a picnic into a first-class affair. Grab something to go and enjoy a bench in a lively square or with canalside ambience.

Sandwiches (*broodjes*) of delicious cheese or ham on fresh bread are cheap at snack bars and delis. You'll find takeout stands selling herring, French fries, and ethnic foods.

Albert Heijn grocery stores (daily 8:00-22:00, bring cash) have great deli sections with picnic-perfect takeaway salads and sandwiches. There are handy locations near Dam Square, the Mint Tower, on the corner of Leidsestraat and Singel, and inside Centraal Station.

Traditional Dutch Cuisine

Traditional Dutch cooking is basic and hearty—meat or fish, soup, fresh bread, boiled potatoes, cooked vegetables, and salad. Mashed potato dishes (*stamppot* or *hutspot*) served with meat and vegetables is classic Dutch comfort food. But these days, many Dutch people have traveled and become more sophisticated, enjoying dishes from around the world.

The Dutch are better known for their informal foods. Pickled herring *(haring)* comes with onions or pickles on a bun. French fries *(Vlaamse friets)* are eaten with mayonnaise rather than ketchup. Popular Dutch cheeses are Edam (covered with red wax) or Gouda (HOW-dah). *Kroketten* (croquettes) are log-shaped rolls of meats and vegetables (kind of like corn dogs) breaded and deep-fried. *Pannenkoeken* (pancakes) can be either sweet dessert pancakes or crêpe-like, savory pancakes eaten as a meal.

For dessert, try *pannenkoeken, poffertjes* (small, sugared puffy pancakes), *stroopwafels* (syrup waffles), and *appelgebak* or *appeltaart* (apple pie).

Ethnic

Since its Golden Age days as a global trader, Amsterdam has adopted food from other lands.

Indonesian *(Indisch)*, from this former Dutch colony, is commonly

Cafés offer sandwiches and other light fare—good for a quick fill-up.

Ethnic treat—Middle Eastern shish kebab.

Pannenkoeken can be sweet or savory.

served as a rijsttafel (literally, "rice table"), a multidish sampler of many spicy dishes and rice or noodles. A rijsttafel can be split between two hungry tourists. Other Indonesian menu items *(nasi rames, bami goreng, nasi goreng)* are also multidish meals. Common Indonesian sauces are peanut, red chili *(sambal)*, and dark soy.

You'll also find Middle Eastern *shoarma* (roasted lamb in pita bread), falafel, gyros, or a *döner kebab.*

Surinamese *(Surinaamse)*, from the former colony on the northeast coast of South America, is a mix of Caribbean and Indonesian influences. The signature dish is *roti* (spiced chicken wrapped in a tortilla) and rice (white or fried) served with meats in sauces (curry and spices).

Alstublieft: Wherever you eat in Amsterdam—at fine restaurants, dim cafes, or the pickled herring shack—you'll constantly hear servers saying *"Alstublieft"* (AHL-stoo-bleeft). It's a useful, catch-all polite word, meaning "please," "here's your order," "enjoy," and "you're welcome." You can respond by saying, *"Dank u wel"* (dahnk oo vehl)—thank you.

CENTRAL AMSTERDAM

Eateries along the spine of the old center, from Spui, Rokin, and the Mint Tower to Dam Square and Centraal Station (see map, pages 166-167).

1 **$$$ Restaurant Kantjil en de Tijger** Lively, youthful and noisy, purely Indonesian, rijsttafels are good values, reservations smart (daily 12:00-23:00).
Spuistraat 291, tel. 020/620-0994, www.kantjil.nl

2 **$ Kantjil To Go** Indonesian takeout fare, split a large box on Spui Square for best cheap meal in town (daily 12:00-21:00).
Nieuwezijds Voorburgwal 342, tel. 020/620-3074

3 **$$ Café 't Gasthuys** Brown café on a quiet canal near Rokin; busy dumbwaiter cranks out light lunches, sandwiches, and basic dinners (daily 12:00-16:30 & 17:30-22:00).
Grimburgwal 7, tel. 020/624-8230

4 **$$ Pannenkoekenhuis Upstairs** Tiny, characteristic perch up steep stairs, delicious pancakes throughout afternoon (Mon-Sat 12:00-18:00, Sun until 17:00).
Grimburgwal 2, tel. 020/626-5603

5 **$$ Gartine** A hidden gem just off the tourist zone, calm and classy spot for a good lunch or high tea (Wed-Sun 10:00-18:00, high tea 14:00-17:00, closed Mon-Tue).
Taksteeg 7, tel. 020/320-4132

6 **$$$ De Jaren Café** Chic, inviting, local favorite near the Mint Tower; upstairs restaurant, downstairs café for light lunch or drinks on canalside patio (daily 9:30-24:00).
Nieuwe Doelenstraat 20, tel. 020/625-5771

7 **$$ Blue Amsterdam Restaurant** Light lunches high above Kalvertoren shopping mall, one of the best views in town (daily 11:00-18:30).
Kalvertstraat 212, tel. 020/427-3901

8 **$$ Van Kerkwijk** Popular, quirky eatery with no written menu—server relays the day's offerings of fresh international dishes (daily 11:00-23:00).
Between Rokin and Dam Square at Nes 41, tel. 020/620-3316

9 **$ De Zeevang** Dutch herring stand just behind the Royal Palace (closed Sun-Mon).
Corner of Nieuwezijds Voorburgwal and Raadhuisstraat, tel. 020/423-4283

EATING

⑩ **$ Stubbe's Haring** Stubbe family herring stand, in business for 100 years, grab sandwich for a canalside picnic (Tue-Fri 10:00-18:00, Sat until 17:00, closed Sun-Mon).

At the locks on Singel canal, a few blocks from Centraal Station

⑪ **Albert Heijn** Traditional, cheaper grocery stores, great deli sections, picnic-perfect takeaway fare, no U.S. credit cards—bring cash (daily 8:00-22:00).

Nieuwezijds Voorburgwal 226, Koningsplein 4, corner of Leidsestraat and Singel, and inside Centraal Station

WEST AMSTERDAM

Charming canals near the Anne Frank House and Jordaan residential neighborhood (see map, pages 166-167).

⑫ **$$$$ Max Restaurant** Upscale Indonesian food with French influences, choose from a short list to assemble a two- or three-course meal, rijsttafel tasting menu, email reservations (Tue-Sun 18:00-22:00, closed Mon).

Herenstraat 14, tel. 020/420-0222, info@maxrestaurant.nl, www.maxrestaurant.nl

⑬ **$$ The Pancake Bakery** Fun and creative menu, lots of hearty savory and dessert pancakes, bar-like scene but quieter upstairs (daily 9:00-21:30).

Prinsengracht 191, tel. 020/625-1333

⑭ **$$ De Bolhoed Vegetarian Restaurant** Serious vegetarian and vegan dinners, light lunches, colorful setting Buddha would dig, big splittable portions (daily 12:00-22:00).

Prinsengracht 62, tel. 020/626-1803

⑮ **$ Café 't Smalle** Brown café serving soups, salads, and sandwiches; good beer, dine or drink inside or on a canal barge (meals daily 11:00 to 17:30, bar snacks after).

Egelantiersgracht 12, tel. 020/623-9617

⑯ **$$$ Café Restaurant de Reiger** French-Dutch cuisine; famous for fresh ingredients, ribs, and fish; good beer, delightful bistro ambience in classic Jordaan scene, no reservations—go early (daily 17:00-24:00).

Nieuwe Leliestraat 34, tel. 020/624-7426

⑰ **$$ La Perla** Humble tables around a busy pizza oven, formal dining room across the street, lively sidewalk tables (daily 12:00-24:00).

Tweede Tuindwarsstraat 14 and 53—take your pick, tel. 020/624-8828

(18) **$$ Kinnaree Thai Restaurant** Modern ambience, delicious, freshly prepared Thai cuisine served by attentive staff (daily 17:30-22:00).

Eerste Anjeliersdwarsstraat 14, tel. 020/627-7153

(19) **$$ Winkel** Sloppy, youthful favorite, hearty plates, borderline-hipster vibe, great tables on square, renowned for its appeltaart (Mon-Sat 8:00-late, Sun from 10:00).

Noordermarkt 43, tel. 020/623-0223

(20) **$$$ Ristorante Toscanini** Popular upmarket Italian place, lively and spacious ambience, great cuisine, dressy crowd, reservations a must (Mon-Sat 18:00-22:30, closed Sun).

Lindengracht 75, tel. 020/623-2813, http://restauranttoscanini.nl

(21) **$ Café 't Papeneiland** Longtime neighborhood perch overlooking a canal, famous apple pie, drinks but meager food—cheese or liverwurst sandwiches, welcoming benches (daily 10:00-24:00).

Prinsengracht 2, tel. 020/624-1989

(22) **$$ Café van Zuylen** Salads, burgers, local standards, Dutch and Belgian beers, scenic outdoor tables right on the bridge (long hours daily).

Torensteeg 4, tel. 020/639-1055

SOUTHWEST AMSTERDAM

Near Museumplein, Vondelpark, and Leidseplein (see map, pages 166-167).

(23) **$-$$$ "Leidseplein Restaurant Row"** Colorful cancan of eateries on Lange Leidsedwarsstraat, more options nearby on busy Leidsestraat (between Prinsengracht and Herengracht); fast, fun, cheap meals.

Just off Leidseplein

(24) **$$ Café Gruter** Classic brown café on a little square, neighborhood hangout in a ritzy residential zone (lunch daily 11:00-16:00, also dinner, open very late).

Willemsparkweg 73, tel. 020/679-6252

(25) **$$ Café Loetje** Rollicking spot slams out beer and good, affordable pub grub, sit indoors or at sprawling outdoor tables (daily 11:00 until late).

Johannes Vermeerstraat 52, tel. 020/662-8173

(26) **$$$ Sama Sebo Indonesian Restaurant** Top-notch Indonesian, local favorite for rijsttafel, casual "bodega" more energetic than formal restaurant, dinner reservations smart (Mon-Sat 12:00-15:00 & 17:00-22:00, closed Sun).

P. C. Hooftstraat 27, tel. 020/662-81460, http://samasebo.nl

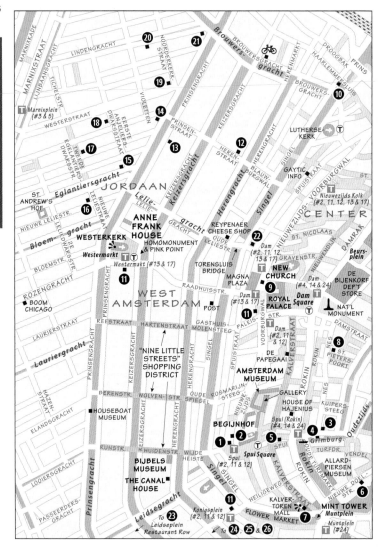

Amsterdam Restaurants

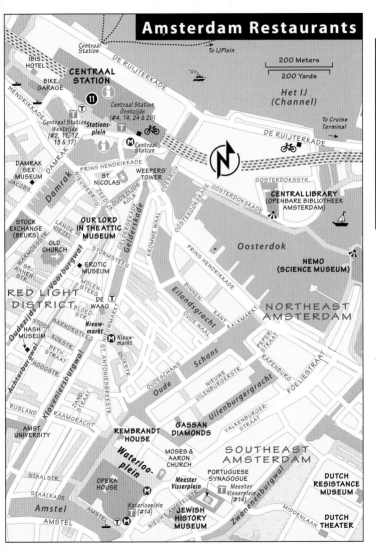

200 Meters
200 Yards

To IJPlein

IBIS HOTEL

CENTRAAL STATION

DE RUIJTERKADE

BIKE GARAGE

Central Station

Het IJ (Channel)

To Cruise Terminal

11

HENDRIKKADE

Centraal Station Oostzijde (#4, 14, 24 & 26)

Stationsplein

Centraal Station Westzijde (#2, 11, 12, 13 & 17)

Centraal Station

DE RUIJTERKADE

OOSTERDOKSSTR.

DAMRAK SEX MUSEUM
JACOBS.

PRINS HENDRIKKADE

ST. NICOLAS

WEEPERS' TOWER

OUDEZIJDS KOLK

ODE-BRUG

OOSTERDOKSKADE

CENTRAL LIBRARY (OPENBARE BIBLIOTHEEK AMSTERDAM)

NIEUWEBRUG

Damrak

ZEEDIJK

OOSTERDOKSKADE

STOCK EXCHANGE (BEURS)

LANGE NIEZEL

OUR LORD IN THE ATTIC MUSEUM

GELDERSEKADE

Gelderskade

STORMSTEEG

KROMME WAAL

PRINS HENDRIKKADE

Oosterdok

WAKNODSSTR.

OLD CHURCH

EROTIC MUSEUM

NEMO (SCIENCE MUSEUM)

ST. ANNEN STR.

Voorburgwal

MOLEN-STEEG

BINNEN KANT

RED LIGHT DISTRICT

DE WAAG

Nieuwmarkt

BLOED-STR.

Eilandsgracht

OUDE WAAL

KALKMARKT

NORTHEAST AMSTERDAM

Oudezijds

HASH MUSEUM

Achterburgwal

STOOF-STEEG

BARNDESTEEG

KOESTR.

BETH-STRAAT

HOOGSTR.

Nieuwmarkt

ST. ANTONIESBREESTR.

DIJKSTR.

OUDESCHANS

Schans

NIEUWE UILENBURGERSTR.

PEPER-STRAAT

RAPENBURG

FOELIESTRAAT

RUSLAND

Klovenniersburgwal

ZAND-STRAAT

RAAMGRACHT

Oude

Uilenburgergracht

AMST. UNIVERSITY

REMBRANDT HOUSE

GASSAN DIAMONDS

VALKENBURGER-STRAAT

STAALSTR.

Waterlooplein

MOSES & AARON CHURCH

SOUTHEAST AMSTERDAM

DUTCH RESISTANCE MUSEUM

STAALKADE

OPERA HOUSE

PORTUGUESE SYNAGOGUE

Meester Visserplein

Zwanenburgwal

Amstel

Waterlooplein (#14)

Meester Visserplein (#14)

MIDDENLAAN

DUTCH THEATER

AMSTEL

AMSTEL

NIEUWE UILENBURGERSTR.

JEWISH HISTORY MUSEUM

Practicalities

Travel Tips

Tourist Information: Amsterdam's main TI, across the street from Centraal Station, is crowded and sometimes inefficient (Mon-Sat 9:00-17:00, Sun 10:00-16:00, tel. 020/702-6000). The TI sells a good city map (skip the poor-quality free one). A second Centraal Station TI, in the new section on the north side (labeled the "I Amsterdam Store"), is much less crowded (Mon-Wed 8:00-19:00, Thu-Sat until 20:00, Sun 9:00-18:00).

Language Barrier: This is one of the easiest places in the non-English-speaking world for an English speaker. Nearly all signs and services are offered in two languages: Dutch and "non-Dutch" (i.e., English).

Shop Hours: Most shops are open Tuesday through Saturday 10:00-18:00, and Sunday and Monday 12:00-18:00. Some shops stay open later (21:00) on Thursdays.

Time Zones: The Netherlands is six/nine hours ahead of the East/West Coasts of the US. For a handy time converter, see www.timeanddate.com.

Watt's Up? Europe's electrical system is 220 volts, instead of North America's 110 volts. Most newer electronics (such as laptops, battery chargers, and hair dryers) convert automatically, so you won't need a converter, but you will need an adapter plug with two round prongs, sold inexpensively at travel stores in the US.

Safety and Emergencies

Emergency and Medical Help: For any emergency service—ambulance, police, or fire—call 112 from a mobile phone or landline. If you get sick, do as the Dutch do and go to a pharmacist for advice (see listings next page). Or ask at your hotel for help—they'll know the nearest medical and emergency services.

Theft or Loss: The city has more than its share of pickpockets—especially in the train station, on trams, in and near crowded museums, and at places of drunkenness. Keep your valuables—passport, credit cards, and cash—in your money belt.

To replace a **passport,** you'll need to go in person to the US consulate (tel. 020/575-5309, after-hours emergency tel. 070/310-2209, Museumplein 19, https://nl.usembassy.gov). If you lose your **credit or debit card,** report the loss immediately with a collect phone call:

Helpful Websites

Amsterdam Tourist Information: www.iamsterdam.com

Netherlands Tourist Information: www.holland.com

Passports and Red Tape: www.travel.state.gov

Flights: www.kayak.com (international flights), www.skyscanner.com (flights within Europe)

Airline Carry-on Restrictions: www.tsa.gov

European Train Schedules: www.bahn.com

General Travel Tips: www.ricksteves.com (train travel, rail passes, car rental, travel insurance, packing lists, and much more)

Visa (tel. 303/967-1096), MasterCard (tel. 636/722-7111), and American Express (tel. 336/393-1111). For more information, see www.ricksteves.com/help.

Street Smarts: Beware of silent transportation—trams, electric mopeds, and bicycles—when walking around Amsterdam. Before you step off a sidewalk, double-check both directions to make sure all's clear.

Around Town

English Bookstores: For fiction and guidebooks, try the **American Book Center** at Spui 12, right on the square. The huge and helpful **Scheltema** is near Dam Square at Rokin 9. **Waterstone's Booksellers,** a UK chain, also sells British newspapers; it's near Spui at 152 Kalverstraat.

Maps: Given the city's maze of streets and canals, I'd definitely get a good city map. You can buy one at the Centraal Station TI. I also like the *Carto Studio Centrumkaart Amsterdam* map. **City Maps 2Go, Apple Maps,** and **Navfree** let you download searchable offline maps.

Pharmacies: The shop named **DA** (Dienstdoende Apotheek) has all the basics—shampoo and toothpaste—as well as a pharmacy counter hidden in the back (daily, Leidsestraat 74 near where it meets Keizersgracht, tel. 020/627-5351). Near Dam Square, there's **BENU Apotheek** (daily, Damstraat 2, tel. 020/624-4331).

Laundry: Try **Clean Brothers Wasserij** in the Jordaan (daily, Westerstraat 26, one block from Prinsengracht, tel. 020/627-9888) or

Powders, near Leidseplein (daily, Kerkstraat 56, one block south of Leidsestraat, mobile 06-5741-2403).

ARRIVAL IN AMSTERDAM

Schiphol Airport

Schiphol Airport (SKIP-pol, code: AMS, www.schiphol.nl), about 10 miles southwest of Amsterdam's city center, is user-friendly. Though Schiphol officially has four terminals, it's really just one big building. You could walk it end to end in about 20 minutes (but allow extra time to pass through security checkpoints between certain terminals). All terminals have ATMs, banks, shops, bars, and free Wi-Fi.

Baggage-claim areas for all terminals empty into the same central zone, officially called Schiphol Plaza but generally signed *Arrivals Hall*. Here you'll find a busy **TI** (near Terminal 2, daily 7:00-22:00), and transportation options: train, bus, taxi, and Uber.

Convenient **luggage lockers** are at various points around the airport (both short- and long-term lockers, cash and cards accepted; biggest bank of lockers near the train station at Schiphol Plaza). To get train information, buy a ticket, or validate your rail pass, take advantage of the **"Train Tickets and Services" counter** (Schiphol Plaza ground level, across from Burger King).

To get between Schiphol and downtown Amsterdam, you have several options:

By Train: Direct trains to Amsterdam's Centraal Station run frequently from Schiphol Plaza (4-6/hour, 20 minutes, €5.30). Schiphol's train station also serves other destinations, including Delft, The Hague, Rotterdam, Bruges, and Brussels.

If you're only going to Amsterdam, consider the **Amsterdam Travel Ticket.** It covers all city trams and buses, as well as the train ride to and from Schiphol (€16/1 day, multiday options, http://en.gvb.nl/amsterdam-travel-ticket).

By Shuttle Bus: The Connexxion shuttle bus departs from lane A7, outside Schiphol Plaza, and takes you directly to most hotels. There are three routes—ask the attendant which one works best for you (2/hour, 20-45 minutes depending on hotel, €17 one-way, €28 round-trip, credit card only). To return to Schiphol from Amsterdam, reserve at least two hours ahead (tel. 088-339-4741, www.airporthotelshuttle.nl).

Schiphol Airport is a quick train ride...   ...from Amsterdam's Centraal Station.

By Public Bus: Bus #397 is handy for those going to the Leidseplein district (€5, credit card only, buy ticket from driver, departs from lane B9 in front of the airport).

By Taxi or Uber: Allow about €50 to downtown Amsterdam by regular **taxi. Uber** serves the airport for about €28.

Centraal Train Station

The portal connecting Amsterdam to the world is its aptly named Centraal Station. From here you're within walking distance of Dam Square, and all the transportation options (tram, bus, taxi, Metro, and rental bikes) are right out front.

The station is fully equipped. Luggage lockers are in the east corridor, under the "B" end of the platforms (always open, can fill up on busy summer weekends). You'll also find plenty of shops, eateries, and "to go" supermarkets. The Service Point store in the north section is a handy place to buy a SIM card, mail a package, or print a ticket (daily 7:00-22:00).

If you need to buy train tickets, ticket machines accept cash (coins only) as well as most US credit cards (with a chip and PIN).

Exiting the station, you're in the heart of the city. Straight ahead is Damrak street, leading to Dam Square (a 10-minute walk). To your left are the main TI, the GVB public-transit information office, and bike-rental places. To the right of the station lie the postcard-perfect neighborhoods of West Amsterdam, within walking distance. Also to your right are taxis.

Trams #2, #11, and #12 all start here (in front of the station) and follow the same route through the center of town with stops within easy walking distance of most of my recommended hotels.

By Tram, Bus, and Metro

Amsterdam's public transit system includes trams, buses, and an underground Metro. Of these, trams are most useful for most tourists. For transit information, visit the helpful GVB public-transit information office in front of Centraal Station (Mon-Fri 7:00-21:00, Sat-Sun from 8:00) or their website (www.gvb.nl). The official GVB app offers route-planning features and real-time updates.

Single Tickets and Day Passes: A **single transit ticket** costs €3 and is good for one hour on the tram, bus, and Metro, including transfers. **Passes** good for unlimited city transit are available for 24 hours (€7.50), 48 hours (€12.50), 72 hours (€17.50), and 96 hours (€22.50). Buy tickets and day passes from machines at most tram stops or on board all buses and most trams. If you buy on board, you can only pay with a credit card (may need PIN; 96-hour pass not available). Tickets and passes are also available at Metro-station vending machines, GVB public-transit offices, TIs, and some souvenir shops.

Regional Transit Pass: The **Amsterdam & Region Travel Ticket** covers in-city trams and buses, as well as trains to nearby destinations such as Haarlem, Zaanse Schans, Edam, Volendam, Marken (by bus), Aalsmeer, and Schipol Airport. If you do two or more day trips, the 2- or 3-day passes can save you a little money and hassle (€26/2 days, €33.50/3 days; one-day pass not worth it); sold at I Amsterdam TIs and stores, and ticket machines at Schipol and in Centraal Station's IJ-Hall (north side); www.iamsterdam.com.

If it's available, the **TripKey Pass** offers discounted, pay-as-you-go travel on local and intercity public transportation. Before you leave home, check www.tripkey.nl for information and updates.

Trams: Buy tickets from machines at the tram stop (coins or credit cards). Or simply hop on, buy your ticket on board (credit cards only), and you're on your way. Board the tram at any door not marked with a red/white "do not enter" sticker. Once aboard, you must immediately "check in" by touching your pass or paper ticket to one of the pink-and-gray scanners. The scanner will beep and flash a green light after a successful scan. Be careful not to accidentally scan your ticket or pass twice while boarding, or it becomes invalid. Just before exiting, you must "check out" by scanning it again.

Trams #2, #11, and #12 travel north-south, connecting Centraal

Get a bike—it's how locals roll.   Trams connect you to many sights and hotels.

Station, the Jordaan neighborhood, many of my recommended hotels, and Leidseplein. Trams #2 and #12 continue beyond Leidseplein to the Rijksmuseum, Van Gogh Museum, and Vondelpark. Tram #14 runs south-east, connecting Centraal Station to Rembrandtplein, Waterlooplein, and Alexanderplein, and Southeast Amsterdam sights. To get to the Anne Frank House and the Jordaan, take tram #13 or #17 from Centraal Station or the west side of Dam Square to Westermarkt.

Buses and Metro: Tickets and passes work on buses and the Metro as they do on the trams—pay with a credit card (may need PIN; no cash), and scan your ticket or pass as you enter and again when you leave. The Metro system is limited and used mostly for commuting to the suburbs—but it does loosely connect Centraal Station with some sights to the south and east of Damrak.

By Bike

You'll get around town by bike faster than you can by taxi. Everyone—bank managers, students, pizza delivery boys, and police—uses this mode of transport. It's by far the smartest way to travel in a city where 40 percent of all traffic rolls on two wheels. One-speed bikes, with *"brrringing"* bells and foot brakes, rent for about €10 per day (cheaper for longer periods) at any number of places—hotels can send you to the nearest spot.

Star Bikes Rental has cheap rates and long hours (5-minute walk from east end of Centraal Station, at De Ruyterkade 143, tel. 020/620-3215, www.starbikesrental.com). **MacBike** has a huge and efficient outlet at Centraal Station as well as two smaller satellite locations (also rents electric bikes, at east end of station—on the left as you exit; tel. 020/624-8391, www.macbike.nl). **Frederic Rent-a-Bike,** a 10-minute walk from Centraal Station, has quality bikes and

Cruise to sights on a hop-on, hop-off boat.   Cash isn't always king—be prepared.

a helpful staff (RS%—10 percent discount, Binnen Wieringerstraat 23, tel. 020/624-5509, www.frederic.nl).

Biking Tips: No one here wears a helmet. They do, however, ride cautiously, and so should you: Use arm signals, follow the bike-only traffic signals, stay in the obvious and omnipresent bike lanes, and yield to traffic on the right. Fear oncoming trams and tram tracks. Obey all traffic signals, and walk your bike through pedestrian zones (fines are reportedly €30-50). Google Maps helpfully includes bicycles as a mode of transportation for the Netherlands. For bike tours, see "Guided Bike Tours," in the Activities chapter.

By Boat

You can also get around Amsterdam by hop-on, hop-off boat. **Lovers** boat lines shuttle tourists on two routes covering different combinations of the city's top sights (€27.50/24-hour pass, roughly every 20 minutes, 2 hours). Most routes come with recorded narration (departures daily 9:30-18:15, tel. 020/530-1090, www.lovers.nl). The similar **Stromma** offers nine stops on two different routes (€24.50/24-hour pass, departures daily 9:30-19:00, until 20:00 July-Aug, tel. 020/217-0500, www.stromma.nl).

By Taxi and Uber

Given the good tram system and ease of biking, I use taxis less in Amsterdam than in just about any other city in Europe. The city's taxis have a drop charge (about €3), after which it's €2.19 per kilometer. You can wave them down, find a rare taxi stand, call one (tel. 020/777-7777), or download their app (Taxi Amsterdam "TaxiTCA"). Uber works in Amsterdam like in the US with your US app; you'll need Wi-Fi or a data plan (pricing based on demand).

Tipping

Tipping in the Netherlands isn't as automatic and generous as it is in the US, but some general guidelines apply.

Restaurants: At Dutch restaurants that have waitstaff, a 15 percent service fee is included in the menu price, although it's common to round up the bill after a good meal (usually 5-10 percent).

Taxis: For a typical ride, round up your fare a bit (for instance, if the fare is €4.50, pay €5).

Services: In general, if someone in the tourism or service industry does a super job for you, a small tip of a euro or two is appropriate. If you're not sure whether (or how much) to tip for a service, ask a local for advice.

You'll also see **bike taxis,** particularly near Dam Square and Leidseplein. Negotiate a rate for the trip before you board (estimate €1/3 minutes, no surcharge for baggage, sample fare from Leidseplein to Anne Frank House: about €6).

By Car

If you have a car, park it—all you'll find are frustrating one-way streets, terrible parking, and meter maids with a passion for booting cars. You'll pay €70 a day to park safely in a central garage. Better, leave the car at one of the city's supervised suburban park-and-ride lots (follow *P&R* signs from freeway, €8/24 hours).

MONEY

The Netherlands uses the euro currency: 1 euro (€) = about $1.20. To convert prices in euros to dollars, add about 20 percent: €20 = about $24, €50 = about $60. (Check www.oanda.com for the latest exchange rates.)

Here's my basic strategy for using money in the Netherlands:

Upon arrival, head for a cash machine (ATM, known as a *geld-automaat*) at the airport and withdraw some euros, using a debit card with low international transaction fees.

Pay for most purchases with your choice of cash or a credit card. The trend is for bigger expenses to be paid by credit card (and some vendors in Amsterdam only accept payment with a credit card), but cash is still the standby for small purchases and tips. Having cash on hand helps you out of a jam if your card randomly doesn't work. Keep your cards and cash safe in a money belt.

US cards no longer require a signature for verification, but don't be surprised if a European card reader generates a receipt for you to sign. Some card readers will accept your card as is; others may prompt you to enter your PIN (so it's important to know the code for each of your cards).

At self-service payment machines (transit-ticket kiosks, parking, etc.), results are mixed, as US cards may not work in unattended transactions. If your card won't work, look for a cashier who can process your card manually—or pay in cash.

STAYING CONNECTED

Making International Calls

For the dialing instructions below, use the complete phone number, including the area code (if there is one).

From a Mobile Phone: It's easy to dial with a mobile phone. Whether calling from the US to Europe, country to country within Europe, or from Europe to the US—it's all the same: Press and hold zero until you get a + sign, enter the country code (31 for the Netherlands), then dial the phone number.

From a US Landline to Europe: Dial 011 (US/Canada access code), country code (31 for the Netherlands), and phone number.

From a European Landline to the US or Europe: Dial 00 (Europe access code), country code (1 for the US), and phone number.

To make a collect call to the US, dial 0800-022-9111. For more phoning help, see www.howtocallabroad.com.

Budget Tips for Using A Mobile Phone in Europe

Sign up for an international plan. To stay connected at a lower cost, sign up for an international service plan through your carrier. Most providers offer a simple bundle that includes calling, messaging, and data.

Use free Wi-Fi whenever possible. Unless you have an unlimited-data plan, you're best off saving most of your online tasks for Wi-Fi. Most accommodations in Europe offer free Wi-Fi, and many cafés have free hotspots for customers. You'll also often find Wi-Fi at

TIs, city squares, major museums, public-transit hubs, airports, and aboard trains and buses.

Minimize use of your cellular network. Even with an international data plan, wait until you're on Wi-Fi to Skype, download apps, stream videos, or do other megabyte-greedy tasks. Using a navigation app such as Google Maps over a cellular network can take lots of data, so do this sparingly or use it offline.

Use Wi-Fi calling and messaging apps. Skype, WhatsApp, and FaceTime are great for making free or low-cost calls or sending texts over Wi-Fi.

RESOURCES FROM RICK STEVES

Begin your trip at RickSteves.com. This guidebook is just one of many titles in my series on European travel. I also produce a public television series, *Rick Steves' Europe,* and a public radio show, *Travel with Rick Steves.* My mobile-friendly website is *the* place to explore Europe in preparation for your trip. You'll find thousands of fun articles, videos, and radio interviews; a wealth of money-saving tips; travel news dispatches; a video library of my travel talks; my travel blog; and my latest guidebook updates (www.ricksteves.com/update).

Packing Checklist

Clothing

- ❑ 5 shirts: long- & short-sleeve
- ❑ 2 pairs pants (or skirts/capris)
- ❑ 1 pair shorts
- ❑ 5 pairs underwear & socks
- ❑ 1 pair walking shoes
- ❑ Sweater or warm layer
- ❑ Rainproof jacket with hood
- ❑ Tie, scarf, belt, and/or hat
- ❑ Swimsuit
- ❑ Sleepwear/loungewear

Money

- ❑ Debit card(s)
- ❑ Credit card(s)
- ❑ Hard cash (US $100-200)
- ❑ Money belt

Documents

- ❑ Passport
- ❑ Tickets & confirmations: flights, hotels, trains, rail pass, car rental, sight entries
- ❑ Driver's license
- ❑ Student ID, hostel card, etc.
- ❑ Photocopies of important documents
- ❑ Insurance details
- ❑ Guidebooks & maps
- ❑ Notepad & pen
- ❑ Journal

Toiletries Kit

- ❑ Soap, shampoo, toothbrush, toothpaste, floss, deodorant, sunscreen, brush/comb, etc.
- ❑ Medicines & vitamins
- ❑ First-aid kit
- ❑ Glasses/contacts/sunglasses
- ❑ Sewing kit
- ❑ Packet of tissues (for WC)
- ❑ Earplugs

Electronics

- ❑ Mobile phone
- ❑ Camera & related gear
- ❑ Tablet/ebook reader/laptop
- ❑ Headphones/earbuds
- ❑ Chargers & batteries
- ❑ Plug adapters

Miscellaneous

- ❑ Daypack
- ❑ Sealable plastic baggies
- ❑ Laundry supplies
- ❑ Small umbrella
- ❑ Travel alarm/watch

Optional Extras

- ❑ Second pair of shoes
- ❑ Travel hairdryer
- ❑ Water bottle
- ❑ Fold-up tote bag
- ❑ Small flashlight & binoculars
- ❑ Small towel or washcloth
- ❑ Tiny lock
- ❑ Extra passport photos

Dutch Survival Phrases

Most people speak English, but if you learn the pleasantries and key phrases, you'll connect better with the locals. To pronounce the guttural Dutch "g" (indicated in phonetics by *h*), make a clear-your-throat sound, similar to the "ch" in the Scottish word "loch."

Hello.	Hallo.	**hah**-loh
Good day.	Dag.	da*h*
Good morning.	Goedemorgen.	**hoo**-deh-mor-*h*ehn
Do you speak English?	Spreekt u Engels?	shpraykt oo **eng**-ehls
Yes. / No.	Ja. / Nee.	yah / nay
I (don't) understand.	Ik begrijp (het niet).	ik beh-**hripe** (heht neet)
Please. (Also: You're welcome.)	Alstublieft.	**ahl**-stoo-bleeft
Thank you.	Dank u wel.	dahnk oo vehl
Excuse me.	Pardon.	**par**-dohn
Goodbye.	Tot ziens.	toht zeens
one / two / three	een / twee / drie	ayn / t'vay / dree
What does it cost?	Wat kost het?	vaht kohst heht
I would like...	Ik wil graag...	ik vil *h*rah
...a room.	...een kamer.	ayn **kah**-mer
...a ticket.	...een kaartje.	ayn **kart**-yeh
...a bike.	...een fiets.	ayn feets
Where is...?	Waar is...?	var is
...the station	...het station	heht **staht**-see-ohn
...the tourist info office	...de VVV	deh fay fay fay
...the toilet	...het toilet	heht **twah**-leht
men / women	mannen / vrouwen	**mah**-nehn / **frow**-ehn
left / right	links / rechts	links / re*h*ts
straight ahead	rechtdoor	**re***h*t-dor
What time does it open / close?	Hoe laat gaat het open / dicht?	hoo laht *h*aht heht **oh**-pehn / di*h*t
now / soon / later	nu / straks / later	noo / strahks / **lah**-ter
today / tomorrow	vandaag / morgen	**fahn**-dah / **mor**-*h*ehn

In the Restaurant

The all-purpose Dutch word *alstublieft* (**ahl**-stoo-bleeft) means "please," but it can also mean "here you are" (when the server hands you something), "thanks" (when taking your payment), or "you're welcome" (when handing you change). Here are other words that might come in handy at restaurants:

I would like...	Ik wil graag... ik vil *h*rah
...a table for one / two.	...een tafel voor een / twee. ayn **tah**-fehl for ayn / t'vay
...to reserve a table.	...een tafel reserveren. ayn **tah**-fehl ray-zehr-feh-rehn
...the menu (in English).	...het menu (in het Engels). heht meh-**noo** (in heht **eng**-ehls)
Is this table free?	Is deze tafel vrij? is **day**-zeh **tah**-fehl fry
to go	om mee te nemen ohm may teh **nay**-mehn
with / without	met / zonder meht / **zohn**-der
and / or	en / of ehn / of
bread / cheese	brood / kaas brohd / kahs
sandwich	sandwich **sand**-vich
soup / salad	soep / sla soop / slah
meat / chicken / fish	vlees / kip / vis flays / kip / fis
fruit / vegetables	vrucht / groenten fru*h*t / **h**roon-tehn
dessert / pastries	gebak heh-**bahk**
I am vegetarian.	Ik ben vegetarisch. ik behn vay-heh-**tah**-rish
coffee / tea / water	koffie / thee / water **koh**-fee / tay / **vah**-ter
wine / beer	wijn / bier vine / beer
red / white	rode / witte **roh**-deh / **vit**-teh
glass / bottle	glas / fles *h*lahs / flehs
Cheers!	Proost! prohst
The bill, please.	De rekening, alstublieft. deh **ray**-keh-neeng **ahl**-stoo-bleeft
Tasty.	Lekker. **leh**-ker
Enjoy!	Smakelijk! **smah**-keh-like

INDEX

Start your trip at

Our website enhances this book and turns

Explore Europe

At ricksteves.com you can browse through thousands of articles, videos, photos and radio interviews, plus find a wealth of money-saving travel tips for planning your dream trip. And with our mobile-friendly website, you can easily access all this great travel information anywhere you go.

TV Shows

Preview the places you'll visit by watching entire half-hour episodes of Rick Steves' Europe (choose from all 100 shows) on-demand, for free.

ricksteves.com

your travel dreams into affordable reality

Radio Interviews

Enjoy ready access to Rick's vast library of radio interviews covering

travel tips and cultural insights that relate specifically to your Europe travel plans.

Travel Forums

Learn, ask, share! Our online community of savvy travelers is a great resource for first-time travelers to Europe, as well as seasoned pros. You'll find forums on each country, plus travel tips and restaurant/hotel reviews. You can even ask one of our well-traveled staff to chime in with an opinion.

Travel News

Subscribe to our free Travel News e-newsletter, and get monthly updates from Rick on what's happening in Europe.

Audio Europe™

Rick's Free Travel App

Get your FREE Rick Steves Audio Europe™ app to enjoy…

- Dozens of self-guided tours of Europe's top museums, sights and historic walks
- Hundreds of tracks filled with cultural insights and sightseeing tips from Rick's radio interviews
- All organized into handy geographic playlists
- For Apple and Android

With Rick whispering in your ear, Europe gets even better.

Find out more at ricksteves.com

Pack Light and Right

Gear up for your next adventure at ricksteves.com

Light Luggage

Pack light and right with Rick Steves' affordable, custom-designed rolling carry-on bags, backpacks, day packs and shoulder bags.

Accessories

From packing cubes to moneybelts and beyond, Rick has personally selected the travel goodies that will help your trip go smoother.

Shop at ricksteves.com

Experience maximum Europe

Save time and energy

This guidebook is your independent-travel toolkit. But for all it delivers, it's still up to you to devote the time and energy it takes to manage the preparation and logistics that are essential for a happy trip. If that's a hassle, there's a solution.

Rick Steves Tours

A Rick Steves tour takes you to Europe's most interesting places with great guides and small groups

great tours, too!

with minimum stress

of 28 or less. We follow Rick's favorite itineraries, ride in comfy buses, stay in family-run hotels, and bring you intimately close to the Europe you've traveled so far to see. Most importantly, we take away the logistical headaches so you can focus on the fun.

Join the fun
This year we'll take thousands of free-spirited travelers—nearly half of them repeat customers—along with us on four dozen different itineraries, from Ireland to Italy to Istanbul. Is a Rick Steves tour the right fit for your travel dreams? Find out at ricksteves.com, where you can also request Rick's latest tour catalog.

Europe is best experienced with happy travel partners. We hope you can join us.

See our itineraries at ricksteves.com

BEST OF GUIDES

Full-color guides in an easy-to-scan format, focusing on top sights and experiences in popular destinations

Best of England
Best of Europe
Best of France
Best of Germany

Best of Ireland
Best of Italy
Best of Scotland
Best of Spain

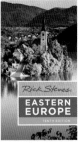

COMPREHENSIVE GUIDES

City, country, and regional guides printed on Bible-thin paper. Packed with detailed coverage for a multi-week trip exploring iconic sights and more

Amsterdam &
  the Netherlands
Barcelona
Belgium: Bruges, Brussels,
  Antwerp & Ghent
Berlin
Budapest
Croatia & Slovenia
Eastern Europe
England
Florence & Tuscany
France
Germany
Great Britain
Greece: Athens &
  the Peloponnese
Iceland

Ireland
Istanbul
Italy
London
Paris
Portugal
Prague & the Czech Republic
Provence & the French
  Riviera
Rome
Scandinavia
Scotland
Sicily
Spain
Switzerland
Venice
Vienna, Salzburg & Tirol

Many guides are available as ebooks.

POCKET GUIDES
Compact guides for shorter city trips

Amsterdam	Italy's Cinque Terre	Prague
Athens	London	Rome
Barcelona	Munich & Salzburg	Venice
Florence	Paris	Vienna

SNAPSHOT GUIDES
Focused single-destination coverage

Basque Country: Spain & France
Copenhagen & the Best of Denmark
Dublin
Dubrovnik
Edinburgh
Hill Towns of Central Italy
Krakow, Warsaw & Gdansk
Lisbon
Loire Valley
Madrid & Toledo
Milan & the Italian Lakes District
Naples & the Amalfi Coast
Nice & the French Riviera
Normandy
Northern Ireland
Norway
Reykjavík
Rothenburg & the Rhine
Sevilla, Granada & Southern Spain
St. Petersburg, Helsinki & Tallinn
Stockholm

CRUISE PORTS GUIDES
Reference for cruise ports of call

Mediterranean Cruise Ports
Scandinavian & Northern European
  Cruise Ports

TRAVEL SKILLS & CULTURE
Greater information and insight

Europe 101
Europe Through the Back Door
Europe's Top 100 Masterpieces
European Christmas
European Easter
European Festivals
For the Love of Europe
Travel as a Political Act

PHRASE BOOKS & DICTIONARIES

French
French, Italian & German
German
Italian
Portuguese
Spanish

PLANNING MAPS

Britain, Ireland & London
Europe
France & Paris
Germany, Austria & Switzerland
Iceland
Ireland
Italy
Scotland
Spain & Portugal

PHOTO CREDITS

Avalon Travel
Hachette Book Group
1700 Fourth Street
Berkeley, CA 94710

Printed in China by RR Donnelley
Third edition
Second printing March 2020

ISBN 978-1-64171-117-3

For the latest on Rick's talks, guidebooks, tours, public television series, and public radio show, contact Rick Steves' Europe, 130 Fourth Avenue North, Edmonds, WA 98020, 425/771-8303, www.ricksteves.com, rick@ricksteves.com.

Rick Steves' Europe
Managing Editor: Jennifer Madison Davis
Special Publications Manager: Risa Laib
Assistant Managing Editor: Cathy Lu
Editors: Glenn Eriksen, Julie Fanselow, Tom Griffin, Katherine Gustafson, Suzanne Kotz, Rosie Leutzinger, Jessica Shaw, Carrie Shepherd
Editorial & Production Assistant: Megan Simms
Editorial Intern: Nola Peshkin
Researcher: Amanda Buttinger
Graphic Content Director: Sandra Hundacker
Maps & Graphics: David C. Hoerlein, Lauren Mills, Mary Rostad
Digital Asset Coordinator: Orin Dubrow

Avalon Travel
Senior Editor and Series Manager: Madhu Prasher
Editors: Jamie Andrade, Sierra Machado
Copy Editor: Maggie Ryan
Proofreader: Kelly Lydick
Indexer: Claire Splan
Production & Typesetting: Christine DeLorenzo
Cover Design: Kimberly Glyder Design
Interior Design: Rue Flaherty
Maps & Graphics: Kat Bennett, Lohnes + Wright